How to Succeed in Accounting Studies

Competency is tied in to respect for teaching,

within the bounds of professional ethics.

AB + Publications

How to Succeed
in Accounting Studies

by

Sylvie Deslauriers, PhD, MSc

FCPA, FCA, FCMA, CPA (FL), CMA (US)

Professor of Accounting

University of Quebec at Trois-Rivieres

Canada

AB + Publications

How to Succeed in Accounting Studies
by Sylvie Deslauriers, PhD

© 2016 AB + Publications

Cover Design: Audrey Morasse
My thanks to:
   Alizada, Christian, Dave, Glodie, Martin,
   Melissa & Pierre-Antoine.

AB+ Publications®

P.O. Box 38
St-Alban, Québec
Canada
G0A 3B0
info@ABplusPublications.com
www.ABplusPublications.com

ISBN 978-0-928067-08-5
(ebook format 978-1-928067-13-9)

Legal deposit: 2016
Library and Archives Canada
Bibliothèque et Archives nationales du Québec

OTHER BOOKS BY SYLVIE DESLAURIERS:

Accounting for Success Guide to Short Case Resolution
   © 2015 ISBN 978-0-928067-05-4
Teaching Tips for Accounting Cases
   © 2012 ISBN 978-0-973803-85-3
CGA = COMPETENCY, © 2013 ISBN 978-0-973803-87-7

PREFACE

Dear accounting student,

Over the course of my various experiences, I have developed a great number of tips and tricks enabling me to adopt a more efficient approach when comes the time to study for, to prepare for, and to successfully write, an examination. Your time is precious and learning how to concentrate on the essentials is a winning attitude.

How can I get more out of what I am doing by expending the same efforts? I am constantly seeking to improve the results achieved by choosing more useful and more appropriate means, namely those that provide a greater added value.

In light of this goal of learning to work efficiently, I also seek out ways to make the learning of concepts more interesting. How can one summarize information in a more visual manner? Or in such a manner as to flesh out the interconnections between topics? And, finally, how can I promote long-term information retention?

I am pleased to share to with you the sum total of my work, in order to assist you in your own success.

Dr. Sylvie Deslauriers

How to Succeed in Accounting Studies

CONTENTS

Part 1: Attending Classes 1

Preliminary Work
Active Listening
Taking Notes
Reviewing Course Notes

Part 2: Studying to Retain Information 15

Planning
The Concepts under Study
Exercises and Problems
Continuous Learning

Part 3: Preparing For An Exam 37

Planning Your Review
Key Concepts
Retaining the Subject-Matter
When to Let Go

Part 4: Passing Your Exams 59

Planning
The Contents of the Answer
Presentation of the Answer
Feedback

Part 5: Working As A Team 89

The Exchange of Ideas
Grading Responses Amongst Colleagues
Written Papers

Part 1
Attending Classes

Preliminary Work
Active Listening
Taking Notes
Reviewing Course Notes

"The learning curve does not move smoothly upwards:
it has its up and downs."

Part 1
Attending Classes

From the outset, I would like to mention that it appears to me essential to attend all classes scheduled as part of your training program. In your learning path, "Attending Classes" is undeniably useful. Your professors are there in order to explain, structure, summarize and demonstrate the concepts. Of course, one must find the means of best using the information provided to you. Do not lose sight of the goal of seeking to understand as quickly as possible the subject-matter of the program.

COMMENT

Some students voluntarily choose not to attend some teaching sessions. Among other reasons, they consider that they can do the work by themselves, thereby thinking that they will save time.

According to my experience, I can tell you that that is rarely a good strategy. On the one hand, a student may postpone what he or she could do as the study session is progressing. However, the subject-matter that has not yet been studied slows down the speed with which one can learn the topics that follow. On the other hand, the individual work required in order to replace a course generally exceeds the duration of the course itself. If one conducts a cost/benefit analysis, one quickly realizes that it is not a good idea.

Finally, one should not count on the fact that all the highlights of a course will be properly relayed to us by any of our colleagues.

Preliminary Work

I suggest that you take the time to plan the courses you will be attending. Knowing in advance the contents of the next course in one's training program is a useful investment. There is, in my opinion, a modicum of work that needs to be performed before showing up for class; this work clearly positions your learning.

© How to Succeed in Accounting Studies

This is what I suggest.

- ✑ ***Refer to the course outline.*** First of all, it appears to me important to visualize the progression of the courses in their entirety. Identifying the unifying thread in the sequencing of the topics allows one to place each of them—as well as their sub-topics—in perspective and in relation to each other. For instance, the various items making up Assets are usually taught in the following order of appearance on the balance sheet: Cash, Accounts receivable, Inventory, Property, Plant and Equipment, etc. Similarly, you will learn how to calculate the production cost of a single product before learning how to allocate joint costs between several products.

    Show the guiding thread of the subjects under study.

    One must also regularly take note of the items covered by each of the individual teaching sessions. This allows you to plan your preliminary reading and promotes the taking of useful notes in class.

- ✑ ***Conducting a preliminary reading.*** One must acknowledge that any student preparing for the next course is faced with new topics that he or she is not yet proficient in. When one shows up for class to take a two-hour course on the accounting of property, plant and equipment, for instance, absorbing the concepts becomes more and more difficult as the course progresses. In an ideal world, it is preferable to read all the material suggested in the course outline before attending class. In practice, it is not always that obvious. However, one should not show up for class empty-handed, on the one hand, so as to ensure that your learning will be the most efficient possible and, on the other hand, to ensure that it will be the most interesting possible.

Placing a topic in an overall perspective promotes an understanding of its specifics.

COMMENT

At the beginning of your accounting studies, I suggest you create a folder or a file containing basic information. This involves grouping in the material in the same location, which can be used for more than one course, or even the entire program.

Here are examples of what such a permanent personal file can contain:

- a complete set of model financial statements;
- a list of useful Web links (e.g. www.ifrs.org);
- basic formulas (e.g. ratios) and discount tables;
- a glossary;
- diagrams and tables that summarize the essentials of the subject at a glance;
- various summaries of the subjects studied.

Prior to showing up for class, I suggest that, at very least, you perform a preliminary reading of the topics on the agenda in order not to be completely lost after some 15 minutes. For instance, before attending a class on fixed assets, one must have acquired knowledge as to their nature (definition), be able to identify that which forms part of the acquisition cost, know that this cost must be amortized and that there are various methods of doing so. You will quickly observe that these are the first concepts set out in the Table of Contents of any financial accounting volume. It does not appear to me to be necessary to know all the Hows and Whys in the most intricate detail. However, by understanding what amortization is, for instance, you will more easily and quickly grasp the operation of the various methods explained by the professor.

Active Listening

Attending classes is a dynamic activity that requires constant mental involvement. It requires more than simply sitting down and waiting for the professor to transfer his or her knowledge to us. Active listening requires training and concentration in order to establish, as soon as possible, the basic premises for an understanding of the subject-matter. The goal is simple: understanding and learning the greatest amount of knowledge in a given time period.

© How to Succeed in Accounting Studies

Here are a few items to consider in order to promote your in-class learning.

- ☺ *Adopt a constructive attitude.* Being positive and willing to learn are the keys to success. After all, you are there since you deliberately chose to be there. When you come to class, consider the new subject-matter that will be taught in that class as an opportunity rather than something you are compelled to do. Have the reflex to use the teaching that is provided to you optimally. In other words, denigration and criticism are a waste of time. Instead, show a constructive attitude.

- ☺ *Remain focused.* Since each course relates to new concepts, one must find ways to not lose sight of the unifying thread of what is being taught. Unfortunately, it happens too often that being distracted, if only for a few minutes, will impede the understanding of what follows. Attending a course without really understanding what is being debated is a no no.

COMMENT
The pace of the course is too slow for you?
You're finding it difficult to keep your focus?
↓
Find something to do!
You can consult, read or annotate the reference volume,
draw small diagrams summarizing the subject-matter
in the margin,
complete your notes taken during the course,
or even answer the review questions appearing
at the back of the volume.
↓
Remain active and concentrated!

P.S.: I am only referring here to the activities relating to your training!

- ☺ *Visualize the progression of the teaching.* It appears to me to be important to examine the manner in which the subject-matter is presented in order to better absorb it. In other words, one must elicit the structure relied on. For instance, understanding the nature of fixed, semi-variable and variable costs is crucial to an adequate determination of the break-even point or of the contribution margin.

It is very useful to identify prerequisites from one topic to the next.

Part 1: Attending classes

> ## Being actively involved in the conduct of a course promotes learning.

℘ *Resolving unsettled issues.* If it is a critical item in the understanding of the subject-matter, one must not hesitate to ask the professor questions. Understanding what being discussed is essential to tapping the full potential of the teaching provided. Any question that comes to your mind must be resolved. Where it is not possible to get an answer during the course or where you deem it to be an issue of lesser significance, write the question down in order to revisit it later. Place a marker at a strategic location, for instance. NEVER leave a question unresolved, because it might very well show up on your exam!

COMMENT

Some students systematically refrain from asking questions because they feel uncomfortable, they are afraid of being embarrassed or of interrupting the class. They sometimes simply have the impression that there is never a right moment to speak up.

On the one hand, I suggest that you think, first and foremost, of your welfare, that is to say your personal learning objectives. You must promote your own success. On the other hand, tell yourself that any question, no matter how simple or absurd it might appear to be, is useful. If it is a key concept, do not hesitate!

By helping yourself, you are probably helping your colleagues as well.

Taking Notes

Notes taken during a teaching session are the basis of the subject-matter you will study later on. One must, therefore, structure them by constantly keeping this usefulness in mind. Incidentally, I suggest that you regularly revisit the form and contents of your notes. Most students passively repeat what the professor is saying or what he or she has written on the blackboard.

While this is assuredly a basic reference, I suggest you adopt a more active approach. First, analyzing what is being taught to you as the course progresses makes your study session later more efficient and, secondly, it allows you to remain more focused during the course.

Here are a few tips that will make taking notes more useful:

- *Identify the topic.* Writing the date, the name of the professor, the topics covered, the relevant pages of the reference volume as well as the number of the exercise performed during the course helps with classifying the information. I especially insist on the necessity of identifying every document with a revealing title and a few key words at the beginning of the text. When comes the time to study, one must not waste time trying to find information.

COMMENT

The notes you take in class are an integral part of your training program. They are read and reread more than once. In light of their great usefulness, I suggest that you anticipate their use as you are creating them. Leave enough room in order to be able to add comments. Change pages when a new topic is being discussed. Adopt an efficient method of classification. For instance, unresolved questions can always be highlighted by a distinctive sign whereas titles and subtitles should always be written in capital letters and in a larger font.

- *Take note of the structure.* The idea is to position the items presented in class in such a way as to interconnect them, and to identify the various parts, prerequisites and interconnections. Emphasize the Table of Contents by using an appropriate nomenclature, such as 1., 1.1, 1.2, 1.2.1, 1.2.2, etc., or a, b, c, etc. in order to better visualize the various steps, for instance. One can also easily underline, highlight or use markers in order to emphasize the main topics.

Ultimate goal? Establish reference points.

1. BUDGETING PROCESS

    1.1 Sales budget

    1.2 Production budget

        1.2.1 Purchases budget   *STEPS*

        1.2.2 Labor budget

        1.2.3 Overhead costs budget

           – Variables costs

           – Fixed costs

    1.3 Operating expenses budget   etc.

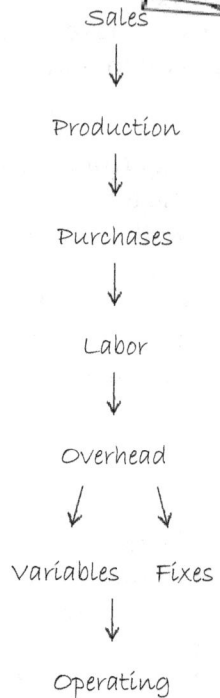

Note the word "STEPS", the indentation in the presentation of the structure as well as the highlighting of the list under Overhead costs.

To the right, a diagram illustrates in a more succinct and visual form the steps involved in preparing a budget. This diagram can be created in class or later on, when studying the topic.

Sales
↓
Production
↓
Purchases
↓
Labor
↓
Overhead
↓   ↓
Variables   Fixes
↓
Operating

In addition to the benefits of promoting learning by structuring one's thoughts, emphasizing the Table of Contents will simplify things when you want to revisit a topic you have already studied. In addition, as already mentioned, this enables you to place the topic in a more comprehensive perspective.

- ℚ *Make the definitions stand out.* Indent them from the margin or write them in a different color. It appears to me to be important to write down the definition exactly as it was given during the class while leaving enough room to rewrite it afterwards in your own words. Personally, I write the definitions of words or expressions on a separate page in a glossary that I create for each subject-matter. That way, I can easily refer to it, even beyond the current course, and learn from the outset to use appropriate terminology at the right time.

- ℚ *Take a step back.* Regardless of the activity performed in the classroom, you must make the most of it. When the teacher asks you to play the role of a shareholder who does not understand the financial statements, try to notice the approach used. This will be useful when you are asked to explain certain concepts.

> **It is essential to be able to
> quickly locate the information you are seeking.**

🕭 *Identify what is important.* I suggest that you conduct a preliminary filtering of the information received by identifying as quickly as possible the most significant topics or aspects. Items of lesser importance or exceptions should be flagged as such. The definition, for instance, of a financial vertical analysis is significant. On the other hand, it is very likely that only the conclusion of an anecdote related by a professor will be noted and identified as such.

COMMENT

Some students write everything they see or hear whereas others jot practically nothing down. It is not obvious how to determine the right quantity of notes to take in class. Not only must each student develop his or her own manner of proceeding, it also depends on the topics on the agenda and on the professor teaching.

One must constantly remember that notes taken in class encapsulate the essentials of the subject-matter and, thereby, become the basis upon which you will later build your studying plan. Choose to take notes of everything that speeds up your learning. If you're not sure of the usefulness of any particular idea, write it down. You can always remove it later.

What is important is knowing how to identify what is important and learning how to collect the information in such a manner as to promote later study. Finally, keep in mind that writing during a course helps you remain focused.

It is certainly not necessary to write down everything that is said in class. Explanations given with respect to an example, an exercise or a problem can be more succinct. In addition, repeating word for word what is written in the reference manual is not always useful. However, never lose sight of the fact that those items that determine the foundation for theoretical concepts being studied are important. You must have the reflex of eliciting and noting the concepts or basic premises in what is being taught to you.

COMMENT

If you happen to miss a few words or even a complete sentence that you deem to be important, I suggest you leave a blank space and continue. You can complete your notes later on by asking the professor or one of your colleagues. You must minimize any time where you are not paying full attention, because you could miss useful ideas.

Remember that it is possible to skip certain words in a sentence without missing the essential parts.

- ℮ *Flesh out the specifics.* It is also useful to highlight the details of the subject-matter itself. Any equation or formula must be identified as such and dealt with separately. Objectives, lists, comparisons, advantages and drawbacks, connections, relationships, etc. must be identified. In addition, diagrams or tables prepared by a professor are particularly useful. If your professor tells you that the "comparison" aspect is significant where you have a financial analysis based on ratios, write the word "COMPARISON" in capital letters in the margin, on each relevant page if necessary. If another professor explains to you that a business may use a perpetual inventory system OR a periodic inventory system, clearly identify that this is a "CHOICE". In addition, pay attention to words that characterize circumstances, such as "NEVER", "RARELY", "ALWAYS" or "COMPULSORY".

- ℮ *Write your personal ideas down separately.* When you are attending class, no doubt an opinion will spring to mind, or you will make observations or ask yourself questions. Good for you! This will enable you to remain focused and involved in your own learning.

For example, indent the information or highlight it in another colour. For instance, write them down in the margin or use a different color. You can validate the contents later. In addition, as mentioned above, any unresolved issues must, at some point in time, be answered.

Where the solution to an exercise or a problem forms an integral part of a course, you are frequently asked to try and resolve the issue by yourself. I know that several students do so using a pencil. In any event, I suggest that you use a different pencil or pen when writing down the right answer. Personally, I would not erase any mistakes that may have been made just so I can remember what was inappropriate. I would cross it out with a giant "X" or I would place the entire text in brackets and take down the appropriate answer.

COMMENT

The notes you take in class are yours. Therefore, do what you must to make them useful and visually interesting. Use abbreviations, symbols, arrows, boxes or circles.
Underline and highlight in various fashions.

Be creative in your manner of presenting the subject-matter!

Make the effort of creating a simple annotation system that will remain constant from one course to the next.

℗ *Take into account the expectations of the professors.* Beyond the subject-matter itself, many professors give advice to their students, which I place into two categories. On the one hand, professors will regularly mention the important topics in their courses and potentially for exams. It goes without saying that this information must be taken into account and highlighted, in the course outline, in the notes you take during class or in your agenda. Knowing, for instance, that the professor expects you to be able to correctly calculate, and then account for, the various commodity taxes during service transactions must certainly not be neglected. A professor may also announce that 25% of the exam will focus on the determination of the inventory cost. Take due note of this information.

On the other hand,—and this is less directly perceptible—, one must take into account the personality of the professor. Two professors teaching the same subject-matter may have different expectations. For instance, it is useful to observe that your audit professor is specifically interested in professional ethics, regularly discussing the topic and always appearing to be interested in debating this issue. You should, therefore, take note of this preference and ensure that you are proficient in the topic.

COMMENT

Professors can also give you good advice, of a more general nature, on how to successfully study. While it is true that most of this advice applies first and foremost to the subject-matter that they are teaching, it may also be useful in other contexts. The manner in which a professor explains how to prepare for an oral presentation, for instance, does not become obsolete once the latter's course is over.

I therefore suggest that you take separate notes, in a notebook or computer file, of these various tips and tricks in order to gather them in one single location. Hence, it is easier to add ideas to the growing list as you progress in your studies and in the experiences you're faced with. Personally, I would collect the information by relevant theme and I would always keep this notebook handy.

Therefore, get into the habit, from the outset of your training program, of proceeding in this manner.

One must promote one's own learning by identifying the most efficient means.

↻ *Be efficient in your method.* Some students resort to various colors, which have their own meaning. For instance, a green highlighter focuses on definitions whereas a blue highlighter identifies important items, regardless of the course in question. You can also create your own pictogram system. What is important is to be able to easily find one's bearings and, in this respect, proceeding in a uniform fashion is an asset.

Each person has his or her own way of doing things, and I respect that.

WHO?
WHAT?
HOW?

However, one must regularly ask oneself if this method is efficient. Realizing, for instance, that one finds it difficult to remember key concepts examined in class may signal that the notes taken during the learning sessions are incomplete. Acknowledging, for instance, that one is wasting time trying to find items that were discussed in class may suggest that it is necessary to change one's method of classifying information. As soon as you note that something is not working well or is slowing you down, identify the cause and find a solution to mitigate or remove the problem.

Do this without delay!

POINT DE VUE

It is common practice for teachers to accompany their teaching with a PowerPoint presentation, for example. At that time, since the slides are usually available to the students, I suggest you use the material offered to you as a starting point.

When using a PowerPoint document, it is possible:

- to add any information directly that improves the content;
- to eliminate pages that do not contain useful information, such as a presentation page, with an "X" in the upper right-hand corner, for example;
- to identify what is important as you proceed.

The objective is to highlight the essentials of the document received and saved it in a separate file.

What do you plan to reread?

Reviewing Course Notes

When you leave class, I would like to stress the importance of re-reading your course notes as soon as possible. The objective, on the one hand, is to ensure that your notes are complete. You must take advantage of the fact that the information is fresh in your memory. Despite what you might think, as time goes by, one slowly forgets what one saw and heard in class. Re-reading one's notes shortly thereafter is an integral part of the information-retention process.

On the other hand, this enables you to draw up a list of the items missing for your notes to be complete. Take advantage of this opportunity to identify the definitions, concepts and ideas that you did not understand. Make sure to settle any unresolved issues, if possible prior to undertaking your study of the following topics.

COMMENT

Some students transcribe all the notes they took in class in a "clean" version. This is an idea to consider, since it promotes information retention. However, this does not mean that it will be appropriate for everyone. Some people absolutely need to write—and to rewrite—in order to understand and retain information. Others resort to other means. I suggest, at the very least, that you consider the possibility of recopying your notes—sometimes only in part—, and determining if this may be an appropriate method for you. On the other hand, I urge those who systematically recopy all their notes to assess whether this is useful under all circumstances. Recopying them only to state that one does so is not necessary.

Obviously, it would not be efficient to recopy one's notes only to improve their appearance. These notes are built for your own personal use; what is important is that you are able to navigate them. It is, therefore, unimportant if they are not as well written or too condensed in certain places.

Part 2
Studying to Retain Information

Planning
The Concepts under Study
Exercises and Problems
Continuous Learning

"The fact of knowing what the aim is, i.e. being aware of the final outcome of the required calculation, focuses one's efforts on what is essential."

© Deslauriers Sylvie, *Teaching Tips for Accounting Cases*, 2012, page 58.

Part 2
Studying to Retain Information

Basically, we want to become accounting professionals. In this respect, it appears to me important to remember that the primary goal of any studying is to learn the subject-matter in order to eventually be able to use it in real life. Obviously, it goes without saying that passing the exams forming part of your training program is essential, but things don't end there. One must "Study to Retain Information" in order to be able to use one's knowledge on the job market. This Part focuses on this aspect, namely the long-term retention of knowledge while helping you develop several methods that will simplify the learning process for you.

I also want to bring home to you that there are consequences inherent in not fully absorbing such and such a topic. Indeed, it may happen that you will pass an exam without having understood one or several of the topics you were evaluated on. However, this knowledge gap nevertheless remains and may no doubt hamper your future success. For instance, those items in the first-year accounting course that you did not fully understand will increase the difficulty you will have in understanding the subject-matter of the second, and so on. One must, therefore, constantly ensure that one has established a solid knowledge base, especially with respect to fundamental concepts.

COMMENT

I frequently notice that a lack of knowledge with respect to basic accounting leads to problems later on, sometimes even until the end of the training program. The impact of the variation of the ending inventory on the cost of goods sold, for instance, is a concept that some students have difficulty understanding. This weakness has an impact not only on certain advanced financial accounting topics, such as consolidation of financial statements, but also on other subject-matters in the program. Hence, the "working capital management" in finance, the "preparation of a production budget" in management accounting, the "calculation of taxable income" in taxation and the "identification of the internal control weaknesses" in auditing require a good understanding of this concept.

> **Fully understanding the concepts today**
> **makes understanding tomorrow's concepts easier.**

One must also realize the ability to make reasoned judgments, to structure and to establish causal links are abilities that carry forward from one subject-matter to another. The more you develop this analytical capability, the easier your learning curve will be later on. In other words, acquiring knowledge will be more efficient as you progress throughout your training program. Do not underestimate the strength of this interaction.

Planning

In order to ensure that you do all that is required, I suggest that you take the time to plan your studying. Whether you do so in writing or make a mental note, defining WHAT to do and WHEN to do it greatly decreases the uncertainty with respect to acquiring knowledge adequately.

Here are the items to consider.

- *Create a stimulating environment.* A key factor to success is knowing how to recognize those things that promote your learning. Some students only work in the library of their school whereas others are more functional at home. My advice is the following: Do not let an uncomfortable situation persist. As soon as something disturbs your concentration, find a way to improve the situation. It is better to work two hours in a concentrated fashion – and to be able to do something else afterwards – than to force oneself to work three hours in an inadequate environment. If the noise caused by the other occupants of the apartment is bothering you, put some headphones on, go study somewhere else or adjust your schedule in order to work during quieter periods.

  If you are able to, plan your study periods in terms of the duration of your exams. If most of them are two hours long, try to study two hours at a time, without interruption. In this manner, you will have gotten into the habit of remaining concentrated during two hours in a row.

COMMENT

Throughout the many years I have been teaching, I noticed that the mere fact of "starting" an activity is one of students' learning difficulties. In other words, "starting" your study of Investments, for instance, is sometimes the greatest hurdle. Moreover, this unwillingness takes on added proportions if it is a topic known to be difficult or a topic that one basically "does not like". Once this hurdle has been overcome, the rest flows rather better that one expected.

Therefore, I suggest, on the one hand, that you should not uselessly put off what you have to do. The longer you wait, the greater the effort required will appear to be. On the other hand, try to identify what could motivate you to undertake the study of a new topic. For instance, choose to do so at the best slot in your schedule. Or else find a personal and original means of motivating and rewarding yourself!

℘ *Spread the learning process out over time.* Studying the subject-matter of the program must take place on a regular basis, week after week. Do not let two weeks go by without studying financial accounting! First of all, understanding the basics of the third course of the session, for instance, promotes the learning of the subject-matter of the fourth, and so on. Also, studying regularly – and not at the last minute – lessens the inherent nervousness at the idea of a looming exam. Finally, it provides you with leeway should something unexpected occur.

**It is not always possible
to find the time to do everything,
but one must find the time
to do everything that is important.**

COMMENT

You need time in order to absorb the subject-matter studied.
Although I cannot personally explain the phenomenon
in a scientific manner, I know from experience that the
passage of time promotes learning. Haven't you found that
you understand the concepts you studied better when you
picked your notes up two days later or sometimes even the
following morning, despite the fact that you didn't study the
subject-matter in the meantime?

Allow your brain the time it needs
to absorb the concepts you studied.

Your brain is working for you, but it needs its space.

℘ *Establish an ongoing plan.* In other words, be flexible and
rigourous. Take a step back on a regular basis and make
adjustments according to the circumstances. Accept change or
unexpected events in a constructive manner. "Adjusting journal
entries" turns out to be a more difficult topic than you expected
initially? I'm not surprised! If so, you should double your efforts
in order to properly grasp the concepts, starting now. Is it not said
that "cramming" on a topic allows you to better remember?

It is important to study regularly in order to have the possibility
of being able to easily incorporate unexpected occurrences in your
schedule.

The Concepts under Study

It is fundamental to know – and eventually to know how to use – the
subject-matter of the program. Personally, I analyze what I am studying
on an ongoing basis in order to classify, structure, diagram, compare
and understand what is going on. In other words, I naturally ask myself
questions with respect to the subject-matter itself but I also focus on the
manner of its presentation.

Here are the items to consider in learning concepts.

℘ *Flesh out what is essential.* All throughout your studies, do
not lose sight of this objective, namely classifying topics and
sub-topics according to their significance. Quite obviously, I
recommend that you grasp the broadest range of subject-matter
of the program that you can, for your personal knowledge and for
exam purposes .

Part 2: Studying to Retain Information

However, in your learning process, one must first of all understand what is essential, if not important, even if you need to refine the details later on. In order to help you sort things out, it may be helpful to consider what the professor has said and to peruse the Table of Contents of the various topics involved.

COMMENT

Some students study everything without distinguishing between major concepts and exceptional circumstances. This does not matter so much if one has the luxury of investing all the time required in order to do so. However, in a setting where your study time is limited, if not unfortunately sometimes too tight, not properly identifying what is the most important may have unfortunate consequences.

Let us assume, for instance, that you are undertaking the study of the accounting topic of "Accounts receivable". This topic, at its core, deals with "the allowance for doubtful accounts", namely the estimation of the collectability of the accounts and the manner of accounting therefor. Those are the most significant aspects. While it may be useful, and even interesting, to acquire knowledge on the internal control or on the management of accounts receivable, this can wait till later on.

It would also not be appropriate to "force oneself" to study the two following methods equally: the determination of the expense based on a percentage of sales and the allowance based on an analysis of the age of accounts. The second method, which is much more complex than the first, requires more time.

COMMENT

I suggest that you read a paragraph in its entirety before annotating it. Otherwise, everything will likely be highlighted in yellow! If the topic appears difficult to you, re-read it a second time, slower, and out loud, if need be.

Your annotations are complementary to your learning process and must enable you to quickly find your bearings in your reference volume. It is, therefore, crucial to go to the trouble of highlighting only key items and important explanations.

- *Annotating the reference volumes.* As mentioned in Part 1, I recommend that you use your reference volumes with the idea in mind that you will be keeping them. They are a precious asset in your training and in your professional life. Do more than just read the words, ask yourself questions and analyze the contents from various angles.

Use your pencil!

Place bookmarks throughout.

The following is an example of a passage annotated while reading.

An Audit of Financial Statements[1]   *OBJ* → *users*   *PP#3*

The purpose of an audit is to enhance the degree of confidence of intended users in the financial statements. This is achieved by the expression of an opinion by the auditor on whether the financial statements are prepared, in all material respects, in accordance with an applicable financial reporting framework. *HOW*

IFRS or ASPE

In the case of most general purpose frameworks, that opinion is on whether the financial statements are presented fairly, in all material respects, or give a true and fair view in accordance with the framework. An audit conducted in accordance with CASs and relevant ethical requirements enables the auditor to form that opinion.

DEF?

1. *Canadian Auditing Standards, CAS 200.3, 2016.*

Referring to the example above, I wish to draw your attention to the following items:

- Only the significant terms are highlighted, within reason.
- The statement "*OBJ* → *users*" succinctly recalls "why" one proceeds to audit financial statements.
- The margins are used intelligently.
- The word "*DEF?*" indicates that one must define what is meant by "true and fair view".

Personally, I would immediately look for the answer to this question, and I would add it right away in my glossary.

Part 2: Studying to Retain Information

**It is insufficient to merely "read" a text.
One must analyze it in order to flesh out its components.**

- One indicates straight away what the term "framework" may refer to, mainly the Accounting Standards for Private Enterprises "ASPE", or the International Financial Reporting Standards "IFRS".

- The fact that the words "material respects" appear twice is noted in order to draw attention to this concept. Since it is a key concept, one could, incidentally, underline it twice rather than once or it could merely be highlighted in another color.

- The word "HOW" indicates the place in the text where it is explained how the audit achieves its goal of increasing the confidence level of users.

- Two small brackets (✓) are used to indicate the standards and rules underlying the audit work.

- The reference to "PP#3" is to slide #3 of the professor's *PowerPoint* presentation.

In addition to the above, I would not hesitate to write, for instance,

- the letters a, b, c in order to point out the three dates with respect to the payment of dividends;

    N.B.: A timeline is also a useful illustration of the tracking of the dates.

- numbers such as 1-, 2-, 3-, etc., in order to list the various stages of the establishment of a work sheet, or to identify the various overhead allocation methods that may be used;

- the abbreviation "ADV" (or "PRO") which stands for "advantage" and "DIS" (or "CONS") which stands for "disadvantage" of being a self-employed worker for tax purposes;

- the calculation justifying the figure listed in the line item Deferred revenues;

- those terms which characterize a situation, such as "superior/lesser", "preferable", "always/never", "greater/lesser than".

- the information that complements any table, diagram or graph provided.

© How to Succeed in Accounting Studies

☺ *Flesh out the connections.*

Personally, I always try to illustrate what I am learning by fleshing out the structure, the steps, the causation, the relationships, the equations, the similarities, the differences, etc.

For instance, once I have read and annotated the paragraph in the previous example (page 21), I ask myself if I am able to summarize the contents in more of a diagram format.

I then draw the following diagram.

An Audit of Financial Statements

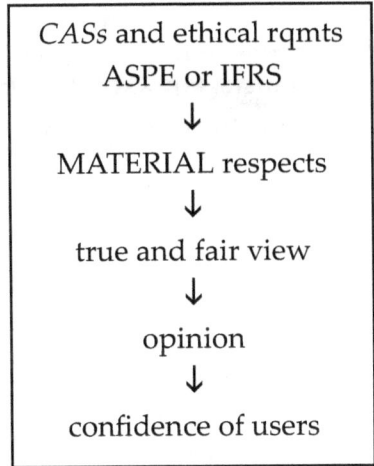

CASs and ethical rqmts
ASPE or IFRS
↓
MATERIAL respects
↓
true and fair view
↓
opinion
↓
confidence of users

☺ *Ask yourself questions.* If there is one undeniable fact that can be taken from the entire advice I give in this volume, it is that one must constantly question oneself and analyze what one is studying. Regardless of the learning activity one is performing, doing so in an active rather than in a passive manner adds value to your training. As soon as you notice something peculiar, repeated, that occurs simultaneously, or that is sequenced in some manner or a connection, take the time to jot it down.

WHY?

Exercises and Problems

It is crucial to do exercises and problems in order to properly absorb the subject-matter. On the one hand, in accounting, speed of execution is important, because time is always limited. It is an inherent feature of the examinations in our profession. On the other hand, understanding the subject-matter – or "thinking" that one understands it – does not automatically mean that you are able to solve the exercises and problems. To achieve this, there is truly no other means that repeating more than once the application of the concepts under study.

Understanding concepts is one thing;

applying them rapidly is another.

COMMENT

Most reference volumes contain a list of short "review questions" at the end of a chapter. Personally, I would try to answer them immediately after reading the text in question in the reference volume. Without necessarily doing so in writing, I would try at the very least to find the answer without looking at the solutions manual. I suggest that you note the questions that you found particularly difficult in order to review them later on, when an exam is looming on the horizon.

The following are the items to consider when the time comes to do exercises and problems.

- *Simulate exercises and problems.* You must really try to resolve the exercises and problems suggested without looking at the solutions manual. It is too easy to tell oneself "I knew it!" or "I am sure I would have properly taken this detail into account!" Without having truly tested your abilities, you cannot be certain that this is the case. Get into the habit of looking at the solutions manual as late as possible in the process.

  It will no doubt happen, while you are solving your exercises and problems, that you will consult your reference volume or your course notes. Refreshing your memory on a concept is preferable to directly reading the solution. Of course, I suggest that you analyze the answer to a given exercise or problem in its entirety before moving on to the next one; this is part of the progressive learning process.

  In point of fact, I suggest that you seek to simulate exam conditions on an ongoing basis. It is not always easy, especially at the outset, but your performance in solving exercises and problems – within the timeframe allotted if it is specified – provides you with useful information.

You must SIMULATE the exercises and problems.

COMMENT

Throughout the process, do not lose sight of the fact that you will have to review the subject-matter later on for examination purposes. Where you encounter an exercise or a problem which reviews the subject-matter especially well, note it.

Some students write it down in their agenda whereas others, for instance, jot down words such as "IMPORTANT", "COMPLETE" or "TO BE REVIEWED" next to the item.

Reference volumes contain a series of exercises and problems dealing with the same aspect of the topic, and generally ranging in difficulty from "easy" to "difficult". Personally, I would complete them in the order suggested in the course plan. Additional or optional exercises and problems can be used where the subject-matter is difficult to understand or during the review prior to an exam. In addition to understanding the subject-matter studied, you must know how to apply it without hesitation; you must be quick in your performance. The planning of your study time must necessarily take this aspect into account, namely the repeated practice of the application of the concepts.

UNDERSTANDING ╋ PRACTICING

↓

QUICK REACTION

↓

SUCCESS

**A difficulty crops up on the horizon?
Turn it into a challenge rather than an obstacle.**

I strongly suggest you solve the exercises and problems in writing, by hand (or on the computer), at least in part and not only in your mind. This forces you to crystallize your thoughts. Practicing in order to learn means that one must do things properly. Take the time, for instance, to write down the description of the journal entries. Do things properly. Write the detail of your thought process; specify where your figures come from. Pretend you are in an exam situation.

The fact that you arrived at the same number as the solution does not necessarily mean that your logic is infallible. It is quite possible, for instance, to obtain a net income identical to that set out in the solution, but to have improperly placed some items in the statement of income. Make sure, on an ongoing basis, that you properly understand the logical path to arriving at the figures in the solution, and analyze any differences.

COMMENT

Many students use worksheets that provide a framework that is conducive to solving exercises and problems faster. Replicating a page from the general journal, the drawing from T-accounts or using a pre-printed work sheet is very useful. It appears to me to be crucial to obtain these templates, among others, in order not to waste any time lining your numbers up in the columns. From a PRESENTATION point of view, this is a no-brainer.

On the other hand, it is tempting to create templates with CONTENTS, in other words, which already contain subject-matter. For instance, some students create a "Bank reconciliation" page where the title of each of the sections, as well as their main components, already appear. I definitely understand the idea that one should be more efficient, but I wish to make you aware of the fact that, as time goes, you may risk not noticing what is written in the template. Come exam time, when you do not have the template at your fingertips, you may find it difficult to determine if outstanding checks, for instance, must be added to, or deducted from, the balance in the bank statement. So, either you rewrite the contents each time or you take the time to re-read it each time, until you have fully absorbed the contents.

(N.B.: The right answer is that one must deduct outstanding checks from the balance in the bank statement.)

ℰ *Learning from one's mistakes.* The following comment may appear slightly strange to you but I hope that you make mistakes during your learning process. (I don't mean on the exam, of course…) In each case, this is an indicator that you should not neglect. Of course, one must understand where the mistake comes from, and identify what is the proper manner of proceeding. If the same mistake occurs more than once, the heads-up you have received is all the more important. For instance, a student who always fails to properly calculate "the amount of the overhead costs period" must definitely get a handle on things. He or she may ask the professor or a colleague for more in-depth explanations. He or she may also, on another day, redo all the exercises and problems dealing with the topic and flesh out the specifics. He or she could also jot down or write out on a separate sheet all the examples of product costs encountered along the way.

> *"There are no doubt weaknesses that I do not seek,*
> *so I must at least take care of those that I do see."*

COMMENT

Some students stop doing exercises and problems on a given topic once they succeed in one error-free endeavor or they "believe" that they understand the subject-matter properly. I fully understand that no one should waste any time performing a repetitive activity with no added value. On the other hand, one must identify those exercises and problems which were not solved, and deal with them as such. On the other hand, I suggest that you briefly look at them nevertheless, by giving them a "glance-through". They may contain a detail that you previously missed. For instance, you might observe that the interest rate in the following problem is quarterly rather than annual.

It would be unfortunate to see this possibility and its impact on the answer to be given, only come exam time!

☺ *Make a statement that you were here.* One can easily understand that the first reflex you have is to compare your own answer to the solutions manual provided. I suggest that you conduct this activity with a pen in hand, using a different color than the one you used to solve the exercise or the problem. Do not hesitate to comment what you have just done. Writing a "Yeah!" or a "VG", for "Very Good", easily underscores your achievements.

Where your answer was inadequate, write next to it what was wrong or missing. Do not erase your mistake; circle it if you want, and add short explanations. Understanding why the answer was wrong helps you understand what an adequate answer would be.

COMMENT

When correcting your own exercises and problems – or even those of a colleague –, it is important to focus on what you must "remember". Whether they take the form of warnings, ideas that you must not forget or a concept that you must highlight, these comments will quickly draw your attention when you review the subject-matter later on. Actually, the mere fact of writing them down may help you remember them.

Here are a few examples of such comments:

- Make sure your book entry balances! DEBIT = CREDIT
- Production cost ≠ Cost of goods sold
- Do not confuse operating leverage and financial leverage.
- Half-year? Do not forget to multiply the interest expense by 6/12 months!
- Investment? Think of the RISK-RETURN relation.

☺ *Go beyond the suggested solutions.* Most students focus only on the numbers – and sometimes even only on the final result – as set out in the solutions manual. They do not take the time to analyze the contents thereof or to read the explanations or comments, if any. I suggest that you do so and also that you reserve some time in order to examine the situation overall. Try, as well, to see beyond the exercise or the problem and to explain the subject-matter in greater detail.

Here are a few examples that illustrate what I mean.

EXAMPLES

Is it possible to prove or validate the figures in the solution?

- The sales price of an item is $15.00. The variable costs are $5.00 per unit and the fixed costs total $5,000.

    What is the break-even point?

    SOLUTION: The break-even point is **500** units ($5,000. / ($15.00 - $5.00)).
    EVIDENCE: Sales (**500** x 15) - variable costs (**500** x 5) - fixed costs ($5,000.) = profit 0.

- Adding the amount of the dividends distributed to the preferred shareholders and to the common shareholders must equal the total sum to be distributed by way of dividends.

EXAMPLES

Is there a different way of reaching the same solution?

- The question states that the sales for the month of June amounting to $200,000. will be cashed in in equal shares in June and in July. The controller considers that 2% of sales are uncollectible.

    What is the amount cashed in in June?

    SOLUTION:

    $200,000. - (0.02 x $200,000.) = $196,000.

    $196,000. x 50% = <u>$98,000.</u>

    ALTERNATE CALCULATION:

    $200,000. x 0.98 x 0.50 = <u>$98,000.</u>

- Earnings before taxes = After-tax profit + Taxes
- Make a single book entry combining the two entries set out in the solutions manual, and *vice-versa.*
- Calculate a capitalized value using a formula or a Present value table rather than a financial calculator.

Getting the right answer is not enough.
You must perfect your understanding.

COMMENT

I urge you to examine the examples above from a purely mathematical point of view. Proving the figure set out in the solutions manual or finding another way of arriving at the same total merely involves expressing the relations from a different angle. Indeed, it is crucial to understand the subject-matter, but considering the mathematical aspect of the relations under study may help you do so. After all, is it possible that the fact that you were "good at math" might be one of the reasons that you considered studying accounting?

❧ *Flesh out the specifics.* I suggest that you proceed as follows: When you have just completed an exercise or a problem, try to identify its most salient features. How is the approach in this exercise or this problem different from the previous one? Since it is rare that you will encounter two problems that test your knowledge of the same topic, in the same manner, establishing what the differences are allows you to survey the various possibilities. Incidentally, it sometimes happens that understanding the exception to the rule allows you to better define the general rule.

For instance, where the question asks you to establish the sales forecast, the information provided may take several forms. Hence, Problem 5 may set out the anticipated sales in terms of quantities and the unit sales price of each of the items. However, in Problem 6, the anticipated sales are set out in dollars and per geographical region. Finally, in light of a production budget already established, Problem 7 asks you instead to reconcile the sales projection figures. Being aware of the various manners of proceeding promotes the development of one's ability to adapt to unforeseen circumstances.

Finally, take the time to classify your exercises and problems. If you have not already done so, write in the margin the statement "easy", "+/-" or "difficult", as well as the estimated time you took to solve each of them. This will be useful when comes the time to prepare for your exams. In addition, as stated above, I suggest that you identify all exercises or problems that summarize especially well the subject-matter or that deal with an aspect that you have greater difficulty with.

COMMENT

Basically, I wish to urge you to take a step back from the exercises and problems that you do. Examining them from a different angle or comparing the approach in one with that used in the other leads to various questions with respect to the subject-matter, which can facilitate a broader absorption of the concepts.

When you have just finished a series of exercises or problems dealing with the same topic, take a few minutes to look at them overall. This will enable you to flesh out the key aspects. For instance, the words "preferred", "cumulative" or "in arrears" must draw your attention as soon as the question focuses on the allocation of dividends between various classes of shares.

For example, you will notice, unless you are informed to the contrary, that payment of the annual insurance premium is entered in its totality in the Prepaid Insurance item under assets and that the term of an insurance contract is 12 months.

Continuous Learning

Learning is an ongoing process. There is always a topic that one does not grasp perfectly or an aspect that is more unclear. Even when you do well on a given exam, you might find that such and such a notion needs perfecting. Accepting this reality as a challenge rather than an aggravation makes studying more pleasant.

Here are a few items to consider in the development of your knowledge.

- *Follow through on your learning.* Leave as few things as possible to chance. All the questions you raise must be answered. Significant topics must be well in-hand. Budget your time in a flexible manner. Try to improve "what is going wrong" as soon as possible, while noting what is going right and what is improving. Be one step ahead!

  In order to study with efficiency, that is to say by reducing the waste of time, I suggest that you get into the habit of noting the information that is of the same nature in the same way. For instance, unresolved issues could always be placed in the left-hand margin and be followed by a large question mark ("?") or be listed on a separate sheet. You could also write out any question, as well as its corresponding answer, in a table with two columns.

> **Not knowing precisely what is going on,
> in and of itself,
> is a source of stress that can be easily controlled.**

In addition, key concepts could be highlighted in a specific color, say blue, whereas explanations of said concept could be highlighted in yellow. The abbreviation "IMP", which stands for "important", could be written in capital letters next to a bracket covering the passage to which it relates. Finally, distinguish between theoretical concepts and their practical application.

I deem it to be very useful to take the time to establish a clear manner of proceeding that will enable you to track what you are looking for in a much easier fashion. Take the time to establish what fits your personal style, and go to the trouble of following through on what you have determined. The stability in your manner of establishing benchmarks throughout your studies will enable you to be more efficient.

COMMENT

One must be aware that some portions of what you read or do when studying will only be read or done once. It is quite possible that the items in question were properly understood or rather insignificant. Personally, when I am sure that this is the case, I jot down a little "x" next to text in question.

I also annotate in this manner exercises or problems that I deem useless to review.

◎ *Make summaries.* As time goes by, you acquire a great deal of information from various sources. You use the documents handed out by the professor, you read your reference volume, and you apply the subject-matter by doing exercises or problems. All throughout this process, you must remember that, at some point in time, you will have to synthesize the subject-matter.

In other words, you must take the time to summarize the topics in order to collect in one single place the most relevant information. Therefore, you must flesh out the crux of each topic by avoiding repetitions and deleting what is useless. When it has been properly done, such a summary then becomes the principal reference document for your study later on.

COMMENT

Given the number and diversity of information sources, I suggest you establish your main reference sources. These documents, kept within reach, thus become the first reference base consulted when any questions arise. Choose credible original references. It is thus preferable to look up the text of the accounting standards directly instead of using a summary found on the Web.

When preparing a summary on a specific topic, I suggest that you consider all at once all the available sources of information. Select the source of information – most often your course notes – which appears to you to be the most useful, as far as highlighting what is important goes. Start your summary by following the structure of this document, and then consult other sources of information regularly in order to supplement the information. Do not wait until you have summarized all that relates to a topic prior to consulting other sources, so as not to be compelled to go back over what you have already done. In your summary, briefly indicate the reference to the documents used. Personally, I place a checkmark (√) or I write "OK" next to the title of the sections that I have summarized.

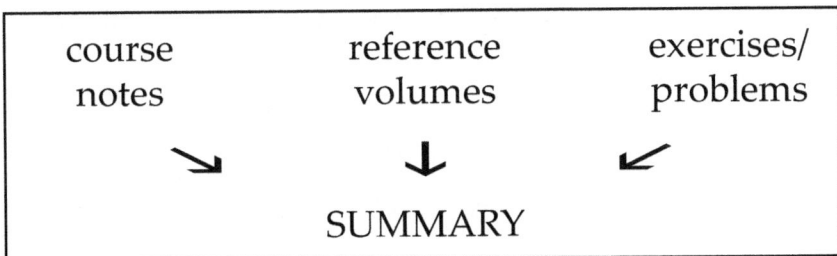

course notes	reference volumes	exercises/ problems
↘	↓	↙
	SUMMARY	

COMMENT

Summarizing the subject-matter of a program is an activity that varies greatly from one student to the next. Some prepare summaries that are nearly as long as the course notes themselves. Others don't do any at all. I stress that the primary usefulness of a summary is to simplify YOUR learning process. Repeating nearly everything that is written in the course notes may help someone who has difficulty with a specific topic. However, at some point in time, you will have to return to this long summary and whittle it down progressively. I would like to add that this manner of proceeding shouldn't be systematically relied on each time. One must adapt to circumstances.

On the other hand, in my view, a student who does summarize the subject-matter is depriving him or herself of a critical stage in the acquisition of knowledge. I am fundamentally convinced that one must at least take the time to stop and take a step back in order to flesh out the key concepts of the topics under study. I will return to this aspect in the following Part, which deals with preparing for an exam.

◷ *Reflecting after an exam.* Course notes, and, in particular, summaries of the subject-matter, are often useful beyond the exam you just wrote. Even if it is not anticipated that this topic will be directly evaluated in the following exam, it is frequently the case that this is implicit. Having a perfect understanding of the difference between an income statement line item and the balance sheet (statement of financial position) line item, for instance, is very useful when comes the time to study accounting adjustments.

I suggest that you develop the reflex of consulting your documents from previous courses. Get into the habit of doing this, as soon as a weakness of your understanding of a topic which you have already studied starts manifesting itself, or simply when your memory reminds you that it can be a forgetful tool.

Mastery of the basic concepts
is essential to success.

COMMENT

Some students systematically throw away their worksheets and note binders one they have completed their session. I never understood this manner of proceeding. Out of experience, I know that it is frequently useful to return to a prior course in order to review or confirm certain notions.

For instance, understanding the nature of fixed costs and variable costs is crucial in management accounting and in finance. If, during the finance course, one realizes that one does not fully understand the topic, one can review the notes one took in management accounting, and *vice-versa*.

In point of fact, one can state with absolute certainty that the financial accounting concepts will be very useful later on, throughout your studies, and even beyond. If you do not understand properly what makes up financial statements, how can you properly calculate the taxable income or adequately conduct a comparative financial analysis?

Believe me when I tell you
that studying with the idea in mind
that learning extends beyond the upcoming examination
changes the dynamics of all that you do.

In the feasibility of what I'm suggesting above, information must be readily available. Indeed, your reference volumes all have a Table of Contents that is easy to consult, which is why it is important to keep them handy. However, I wish to underscore the fact that the documents you have created – personal notes and summaries – are very precious. They must be easily available and could even be, for the time being, pinned to your noteboard.

In order to find them easily, you must be meticulous in the way you classify information. Ideally, you should place the course outline, the documents distributed by the teacher, the course notes and the summaries, in chronological order, in the same folder. It is also possible to digitally scan handwritten documents.

Personally, I would classify these documents per course, in one and the same file, which stands out on the desktop of my computer.

Part 3
Preparing For An Exam

Planning Your Review

Key Concepts

Retaining the Subject-Matter

When to Let Go

*"One must discover means
in order to remember the key theoretical concepts."*

Part 3
Preparing For An Exam

The assessment of performance by way of tests and exams is an inherent feature of any accounting training program. Learning to prepare for this reality as soon as possible and efficiently is a very good investment.

Planning Your Review

I draw your attention to the fact that I am using the word "review" here. This is because I consider that the subject-matter of the examination has been – at least for the most part – previously studied. You now have to schedule the time necessary to review and perfect your knowledge in order to achieve a better result.

Here are a few items to consider when "Preparing For An Exam".

℃ *Draw up a list of things you need to know.* First of all, ensure that you have all the information handy that is necessary to prepare your review. Check in your agenda or in your course notes what the subject-matter to be assessed at the examination will be. If your professor, for instance, mentioned that Problem #5 is an accurate representation of a bank reconciliation, there is no doubt that you must review this problem, – without learning it by heart! Also, if he or she stated that "cash management" will not be on the exam, you must set this topic aside.

OBJECTIVES
↓
MEANS
↓
RESULTS

If need be, confirm the information you have in order not to waste any time; this time is all the more precious as an examination looms on the horizon.

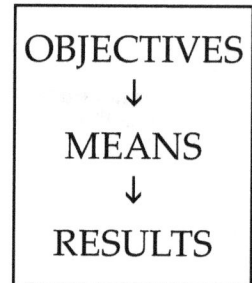

COMMENT

When comes the time to prepare for an exam, some students throw themselves into their review without having sufficiently planned what they intend to do. Hence, they spend too much time on a topic of lesser significance or on a topic that they enjoy more. Or worse yet, some students spend too much time on topics they already know well because they are in their comfort zone.

However, in order to be successful in one's examination, it is crucial to properly understand first what is important. One must also determine objectively what are the weaknesses one must correct or at least minimize. A student, for instance, who knows that he or she is not sufficiently quick in preparing a bank reconciliation must find a way of mitigating this weakness. He or she must practice more or find some gimmick in order to be able to determine the components faster.

REVIEWING notions already studied reinforces your understanding.

I suggest that you take the time to write down the list of "things to do" as part of your review. Break what you have to do down into several more specific parts. Plan the topics to be reviewed, the exercises and problems to solve as well as the summaries to create. Clearly identify what is crucial and flag the topics with which you are experiencing difficulty. Establish priorities as soon as you can. Also, give some thought to diversifying the various learning methods. For instance, do one part by hand and another on the computer. Alternate between theory and practice.

Personally, I always place my study outline conspicuously in order to cross things off as I complete them.

It is more motivating!

ACCOUNTING EXAM NOVEMBER 1

...

CASH

- Bank reconciliation   90 min.

        Review components

        Redo Exercise 3

        Redo Problem 5   IMP

        Review the errors correction   !!!

        Create summary + Learn the structure

- Petty Cash   20-30 min.

        Review Exercise 7 (replenishment journal entry!) ***

...

N.B.: Since it is a personal plan, it can certainly contain more abbreviations. E.g.: "ACCT" which stands for "ACCOUNTING", "PC" which stands for "Petty Cash", etc.

Using the example above, I wish to draw your attention to the following items:

- In order to properly target the task to be performed, each thing to be done begins with a verb in the infinitive.

- In order to plan sufficient time in order to prepare for the exam, the time required in order to complete each part is estimated.

- In order to avoid forgetting anything important or to draw your attention, several signs are used, such as "!!!" or "IMP" or "***".

℘ *Plan for sufficient time.* Stack the odds in your favor by writing down in your schedule the time required for an adequate preparation. Expect the unexpected! In other words, leave yourself some leeway by not planning your study in a timeframe that is so tight that it ends barely 15 minutes prior to the exam. Under such circumstances, part of the review will automatically be glossed over as soon as something unexpected occurs.

COMMENT

I know that some students wait till the last minute to study for the exam that is to take place the next day, even if it is generally known that this is not a good strategy. Under some circumstances, a student may indeed still pass the exam. However, this manner of proceeding has several drawbacks. First, the stress factor is greatly increased, especially since one cannot be certain of being able to grasp what is essential in a restricted timeframe. Under these conditions, one can definitely state that learning is slower and not as good, which, incidentally, increases the uncertainty of successfully passing the exam.

Secondly, any subject-matter that is learned on an accelerated basis is also quick to be forgotten. The learning process does not end on the date of the examination and, as previously mentioned in this volume, any subject-matter that has not been understood is now likely to severely jeopardize your understanding of what follows. In other words, the time you do not invest now, you will be required to make up later.

COMMENT

I know that some students prefer to get up early to study on the very day of the exam. If you are among those students, for the reasons referred to above, I recommend that you not wait until that time to study anything essential.

Do one last overview? YES.

Start studying a new topic? NO.

**You must find the perfect time
in order to review the subject-matter:
not too far in advance
and not at the last minute.**

In spite of the above, I know full well that it sometimes happens that a student does not adequately plan his or her schedule and, consequently, does not, under the circumstances, have the possibility of studying or reviewing the subject-matter in full which will be assessed on the exam. If you are caught up in this type of situation, consider the following: you are better off knowing 70% of the four significant topics than 100% of the first two only.

℘ *Get help if need be.* You must especially not hesitate in clarifying anything that you do not understand. Ask your professor or your colleagues. There is no such thing as a stupid or useless question and you should know that very frequently something that is not understood is right there on the exam. If you are uncomfortable with a face-to-face discussion, send an email. Where teaching assistance periods are scheduled, take advantage of them. Out of experience, I can tell you that even the best of students in class say stupid things from time to time. No one is embarrassment-proof.

DIRECTED QUESTION ↓ EXPLICIT ANSWER

I suggest that you consistently try to narrow down your questions. For instance, stating "I don't understand anything to do with measurement of inventories" is too broad a question. Take the time to study the topic on your own in order to specifically identify which part you do not understand. For example, it is more concrete to say "I don't understand what "non-interchangeable items" means."

COMMENT

Sometimes additional teaching sessions are scheduled. During these sessions, which are essentially optional, the solution to one or two problems that are especially integrating is generally presented. I consider that one should automatically take advantage of this possibility of reviewing the subject-matter using the problem selected by the professor. These problems are usually reflective of one or several of the questions on the exam.

Key Concepts

When preparing for an examination, one must constantly seek to flesh out key concepts. At this stage, one must be able to distinguish items forming part of the subject-matter from explanations and applications of the subject-matter itself. And it is only by taking a step back that one is able to determine the general threads of the topics under study.

- ✐ *Review exercises and problems.* It is important to be quick in the resolution of an exercise or problem. Understanding the subject-matter, describing how to apply it or having all the time needed in order to do so is one thing, being able to solve an exercise or a problem quickly is quite another. Do not count on the possibility of there being any time available on the exam to reflect at greater length, to review or to fine-tune your answers. This does not happen often.

  It is, therefore, crucial to review some exercises and problems, on the one hand to ensure that you grasp the subject-matter properly and, on the other hand, to improve your speed of performance. If, so far, you have not done so, it is now time to solve some problems or exercises that are especially complete, while staying within the suggested time limits as much as possible. For the remainder of exercises or problems, you can simply validate your understanding by going through the process in your head, and then comparing your logic with that of the solutions manual.

> **COMMENT**
>
> Some students learn "by heart" one or two "model" exercises or problems. I certainly do not recommend this approach, which, to me, appears to be much too risky. Retaining information without understanding it, and then applying it without judgment, is a manner of proceeding that no longer works once the question is asked in a different manner.

It is certainly not necessary to review all the exercises and problems set out in the course outline. Choose those that truly incorporate the subject-matter, namely those you have identified as such during your preliminary study. They are usually the exercises or problems with a higher degree of difficulty. Go through the notes you took on each of them in order to remember the specifics of the topics under study. Above all, do not take it for granted the exam will be easy, even if the teacher implied that it would be.

COMMENT

Sometimes, professors distribute extra exercises or they make available to you one or two former exams. If so, do not hesitate to use this material. Conduct a simulation of the same duration as the exam itself. Study the proposed solution in detail.

If you do not have access to such materials, try to obtain information from your colleagues who are further along in the same training program as yours. Knowing, for instance, that such and such professor usually asks you to prepare the statement of income for two levels of production in part *(a)* and then asks you, in part *(b)*, to compare them, is definitely something to be considered. While it is true that obtaining this information is no guarantee that your exam will be the same, you must, at the very least, be prepared. You can learn, in this manner, that the examinations of the professor generally contain five questions, including two that are more difficult than the others. This enables you to adjust your examination strategy accordingly.

**Optimizing one's learning process
guarantees success
well beyond passing an exam.**

Ⓠ *Approach the subject-matter from a different angle.* I urge you to seek original and different ways of reviewing the subject-matter. Use your imagination in a constructive manner. This makes your studying more interesting, it strengthens the skills and knowledge you have already acquired and completes your understanding. Hence, you will be in a position to react promptly to any new or different situation that you might face on the exam.

Here are a few examples of what I mean.

Flesh out the causal connections.

EXAMPLES

Use arrows in order to establish causal relations or to identify the unifying thread. Think of the word THEREFORE which enables you to express the consequences flowing from one item to the next.

bankruptcy of a client → uncollectible amount
→ writing-off of a client account

high fixed costs → high break-even point

taxes collected → to be remitted to the government
→ liability

Crunch numbers.

EXAMPLES

Examine what is going on using algebraic equations and see the connections between the various items. This will enable you to understand connections between the various components and to properly establish an unknown variable using others.

Sales – Variable costs = Contribution margin
↓
Contribution margin – Fixed costs = Net income

AND

Sales – Cost of goods sold (variable and fixed production costs)
= Gross margin
↓
Gross margin – other costs (other than production) = Net income

Examining the information in the form of equations enables you, on the one hand, to better distinguish concepts such as Contribution margin and Gross margin and, on the other hand, to be able to determine, by way of subtraction, the total of fixed costs, for instance.

Do things in reverse sequence.

EXAMPLE

Examine the manner in which things occur by following a different path. Instead of following the usual path, where you start from point A to go to point C by going through B, do the reverse. In so doing, you will very often manage to establish different means of arriving at the same result.

> Asking oneself what the total of the line item Deferred revenues on the balance sheet allows you to determine, or at least to validate, the amount appearing under adjustment entry.

COMMENT

In this Part, the tips and advice I am giving you will simplify your preparation for exams. Of course, nothing prevents you from using any of them throughout your study.

Incidentally, I would like to tell you that you should try to learn to like what you are doing. The task of acquiring new knowledge is greatly simplified when you do so with pleasure. Therefore, try to identify what manners of proceeding you like best and help you remain concentrated. Personally, I really like expressing notions that I am studying using various types of diagrams. While helping me better learn, this keeps me more interested.

Flesh out the operating

EXAMPLES

Explain relations in the following manner:

"**Where there is…, think of…**"

> **Where there is** a debt redemption,
>
> **think of** first recognizing the accrued interests.
>
> **Where there is** a disposition of investments,
>
> **think of** the tax rules on capital gains.

Break down the subject-matter.

EXAMPLES

- Flesh out the steps, components, stakes as well as relations.
  - Draw a timeline in order to better visualize what is going on.
    - Compare methods and definitions.
      - Make associations.

> All the line items under Assets have this in common: they are initially recorded at their acquisition cost, plus direct costs.

> Considering the half-year rule, the capital cost allowance for tax purposes is generally less than the accounting depreciation, in the year of acquisition of an asset.

COMMENT

The learning tips I am suggesting to you in this Part may be performed in various manners. Some students explain the subject-matter to themselves by voicing it out loud. Others write down what they are learning as they are learning it, and not always in a clear and ordered fashion. Finally, some students buy a board, which they hang up on the wall in order to study while standing. In this manner, they are able to solve exercises and problems, create tables, or diagrams, which they then copy out – or not – in a clean copy once they are finished.

℘ *Completing one's summaries.* The ideal summary contains the crucial components of the concepts presented in a clear, logical and concise manner. Generally speaking, a summary prepared at the outset of the study of a given topic is longer than a summary prepared later on. In point of fact, the further one progresses in one's study, the greater our capacity to identify key concepts. This is the reason why I suggest that you review your summaries as part of your preparation for an exam. You can underline important items or simply create a more succinct summary.

Part 3: Preparing For An Exam

Personally, I avoid, to the extent possible, summarizing the subject-matter in long run-on sentences. I also try to find various means of presenting the information. I build tables, I draw diagrams and make drawings or I convey the items in list format.[1]

To the extent possible, I try to summarize a given topic on a single page. In this way, I can, at a glance, see everything that is essential. I regularly place these pages in a conspicuous manner on my noteboard. This stimulates my photographic memory!

**A short visual summary
helps you remember the subject-matter.**

COMMENT

It is certainly useful to examine tables, drafts, drawings or other diagrams already provided in your reference volumes. A table which, for instance, sets out the list of components of a bank reconciliation may even be borrowed in that form. A photocopy of a page of the volume you have purchased is easy to carry around. Some students collect together in the same place all summary tables of the subject-matter of the program.

However, I suggest that you should do most of the creating yourself since it is a significant topic. You can certainly use the framework provided for you as a starting point and add your own explanations. Incidentally, I strongly suggest that you add examples of what may be contained under each of the components of the bank reconciliation. It is not always easy, for instance, to determine if the correction of error is to be added to, or subtracted from, the balance of the Cash line item.

---

1 When the summaries are created on a computer, they can be easily classified, accessed and updated. This can also be placed in the folder containing your basic information. (re: p. 4)

The following is an illustration of a table created in order to show in a comparative manner the difference between capital expenditures and operating expenses. As exercises and problems were solved, examples were added in order to illustrate the concepts.

PROPERTY, PLANT AND EQUIPMENT COSTS INCURRED *AFTER* THE ACQUISITION[1]	
ENHANCE SERVICE POTENTIAL ↓ BETTERMENT (future economic benefits > 1 year) ↓ **CAPITAL EXPENDITURES**	MAINTAIN SERVICE POTENTIAL ↓ MAINTENANCE / REPAIR short life ↓ **OPERATING EXPENSES**
DT – ASSET (or ↓ accumulated amortization in the event of replacement of a part*) √ Physical output increased: E.g.: expansion of a plant √ Operating costs lowered: E.g.: automation of an assembly line √ Quality of output improved: E.g.: adding an electronic measuring system √ Life extended: E.g.: Replacement of the motor of a truck* E.g.: significant repairs of equipment	**DT – EXPENSE** Income statement Examples: – Monthly cleaning of the plant – Painting the head office – MAINTENANCE (oil change) – Minor repairs
JUDGMENT – ADAPTING TO CIRCUMSTANCES – SEE **WHY** COSTS HAVE BEEN INCURRED – ⟶ **SIGNIFICANCE** OF THE AMOUNTS INVOLVED ←	

1 *Accounting standards for private enterprises, 3061.14, 2016.*

It is also possible that this previous table would result from a longer summary prepared while reading the reference volume. Some students could proceed in this manner, especially where they find the subject-matter difficult. For others students, directly building the table below could be sufficient.

Here are other examples of tables that you could create.

ITEM	Definition	DT/CT	Financial statement
...	...	...	...

RESPONSIBILITY CENTRE	Revenue centre	Cost centre	Profit centre	Investment Centre
Accountability				
Examples				
Advantages				
Disadvantages				
Performance measurement – Manager				
Performance measurement – Division				
Transfer price				
Etc.				

- ℰ *Creating info-cards.* As part of your final preparation for an exam, you must find ways of remembering the subject-matter and being able to access it in a timely fashion. I suggest you create what I call info-cards; these cards show the subject-matter studied at a glance. The idea is to build brief checklists made up of only several keywords. In other words, info-cards are cards that focus on the essential concepts of a topic.

SUMMARIES
↓
KEY CONCEPTS
↓
INFO-CARDS

I know that not all students get into the habit of preparing summaries of the subject-matter studied. The length and contents of these summaries may, incidentally, greatly vary from one to the next, from one topic to the next.

It is up to you to study
in the manner that suits you.

However, I urge you to experiment with various methods of proceeding in order to determine which is the most efficient.

Regardless, I strongly recommend that you create info-cards. Go to the trouble of stepping back and canvassing in a succinct and organized manner key notions underlying the significant topics under study. Based on the table set out on page 49, here is an example of an info-card that you can build.

PROPERTY, PLANT AND EQUIPMENT COSTS INCURRED <u>AFTER</u> THE ACQUISITION	
BETTERMENT ↓ ENHANCE SERVICE	MAINTENANCE / REPAIR ↓ MAINTAIN SERVICE
physical output increased operating costs lowered quality of output improved life extended	
↑ ASSET (or ↓ accumulated amortization)	EXPENSE
JUDGMENT SIGNIFICANCE OF AMOUNTS	

N.B.: Some words could be even further abbreviated.

> One must constantly seek
> the most efficient means
> of attaining the result sought to be achieved.

COMMENT

Since they recall in such a few select words what the key concepts of a topic are, info-cards are a very efficient memorization tool. They contain what you need in order to quickly refresh your memory. For instance, you may have summarized, in a table, the features of debt financing and of equity financing.

Having created a reference tool, which, in addition, is comparative, you will find the application of concepts to be much easier to do during the exam.

Here is another example of an info-card:

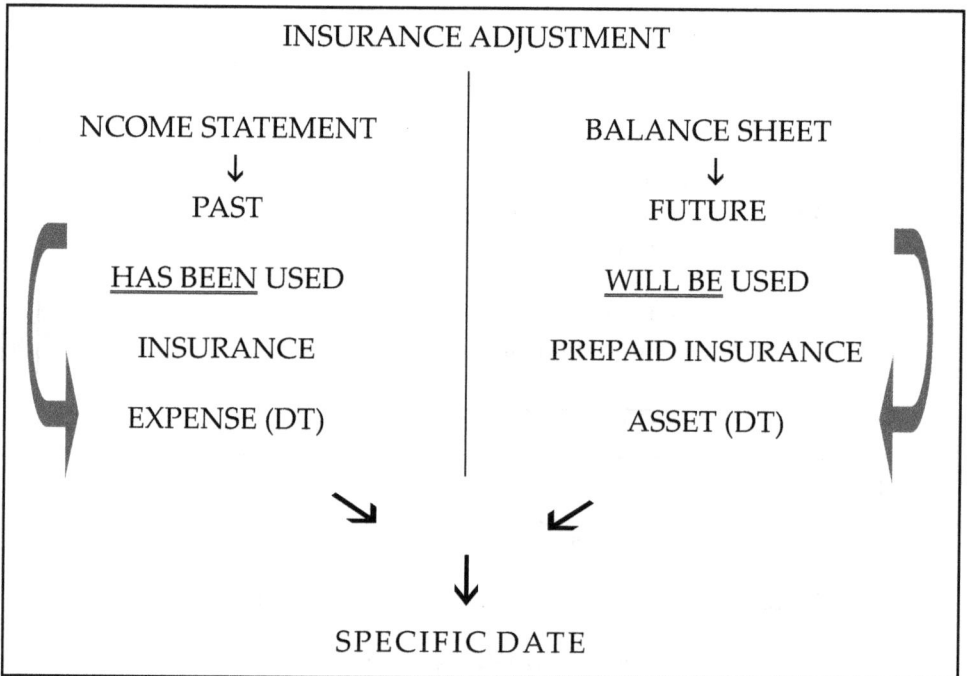

INSURANCE ADJUSTMENT	
NCOME STATEMENT ↓ PAST HAS BEEN USED INSURANCE EXPENSE (DT)	BALANCE SHEET ↓ FUTURE WILL BE USED PREPAID INSURANCE ASSET (DT)

↘ ↙

↓

SPECIFIC DATE

© How to Succeed in Accounting Studies

The above info-card revisits the basic concepts of insurance accounting. It sets out the reasoning leading to a determination of the adjustment entry of the Insurance and Prepaid insurance items. Some students may wish to add a numeric example by way of illustration. One must, however, recall that, on the day before an exam, summaries must be succinct.

Finally, let us mention that the basic framework set out above is fundamental. The logic illustrated also applies to the accounting of supplies.

COMMENT

Most students create their info-cards by hand, simply because writing the concepts out helps them remember.

Some of them write them out on cards *per se*, namely small cardboard cards (3" X 5"), quite simply because it forces them to flesh out the highlights of a given topic.

Since they're easy to carry around, info-cards can be quickly referred to. They can be classified per subject-matter, once the exam is over by using the same sequencing as the chart of accounts, for instance. Having handy the summary of the key concepts of all the topics studied in financial accounting since the beginning of one's studies is very useful. Similarly, various methods of financing studied in finance can be sequenced according to a temporal horizon (e.g.: credit line prior to the trade bill) or according to financial risk (e.g.: the mortgage loan payable prior to bonds).

If you prefer, creating a computerized file containing your various info-cards can, of course, achieve the same objectives.

The advantage is being able to easily find what one is looking for using keywords.

What should one refer to just before the exam? The info-cards!

Retaining the Subject-Matter

Remembering the subject-matter so that it is accessible at the right time during the examination is crucial to success. As mentioned previously, understanding the subject-matter is one thing, remembering it and being able to use it quickly, at the right time, is quite another. From experience, I can tell you that it is often useful to give a meaning to your memories and associate your knowledge with various situations. In other words, establish explicit reference points – expressed verbally, if necessary – that facilitate access to information.

Here are a few tips that will help you remember the subject-matter under study.

- *Visualize the subject-matter.* As discussed above, preparing tables, diagrams and drawings, and then info-cards is very useful. Most students clearly visualize in their head, at the appropriate time, the documents they prepared in this manner. Is it not said that a picture is worth a thousand words?

  Some students even use real or unusual situations to illustrate the key concepts. Thus, the Insurance account adjusting entry can be established by illustrating the passage of time with chocolate bars.

  Make analogies. Observe, for instance, that updating depreciation is the first step to perform when the costs are incurred after the date of acquisition of a fixed asset AND also upon disposition of a fixed asset. The same goes for intangibles assets.

  Give yourself reference points in the resolution of a model exercise or problem.

  Create protocols in this manner.

- *Find your own gimmicks.* Do not be afraid of inventing gimmicks that can help you remember the subject-matter studied. Sometimes, it is the "weirdest" gimmicks that work the best. Some underline keywords two or three times in their summaries with different colors. Others rewrite their summaries. Why not?

  Take the time to determine the items you have difficulty with and seek to minimize the weakness you have identified. For instance, a student that has difficulty with numbers shown as a percentage may simply divide them by 100 in order to be better able to grasp what is going on. What is important is reaching the goal.

  Here are a few tricks which I have used myself or which I have obtained from students I have met over the years.

Think of an alphabetical order.

A student who couldn't remember that **Arrears** of dividends must be distributed before **Cumulative** dividends for the current period told himself that the letter **A** came before the letter **C**.

Think of the amount of information that is necessary.

One student who always forgot to consider one or several of the necessary items in the calculation of the interest expense told herself that there were THREE that she needed to find:

(1-) the amount of the loan x (2-) interest rate x (3-) the period

Since she systematically looked for three items of information in any examination question, she never again forgot to consider the number of months/days in her calculation.

Create a sequence of letters or a word that summarizes the situation.

An intangible asset arising from development must be recognized for if, and only if, an entity is able to demonstrate the following six conditions:[1]

R: Resources are available: technical, financial and other
A: Ability to use or sell
F: technical Feasibility of completing - available for use or sale
F: Future economic benefits (existence of a market)
I: Intention to complete - use or sell
A: Ability to measure reliably the expenditure attributable

RAFFIA

1. *International Financial Reporting Standards,* IAS 38.57, 2016.

Playing with the meaning of words or words themselves.

GOODWILL → GOOD → is worth more than…
→ POSITIVE

FLEXIBLE BUDGET → which is adaptable
→ which VARIES according to production volume

DEcreasing charge method → DEcreases over time

Think about journal entries or T-accounts.

In order to understand what is going on, I regularly use the Cash item as a reference. For instance, in order to determine the impact of a debt redemption on a balance sheet, I ask myself this question: what is the impact on the Cash item? It is a cash outflow, therefore a credit. On the other hand, the Debt item is debited and therefore reduced. This trick was particularly useful at the beginning of my accounting studies.

If, for instance, you have trouble figuring out that an increase of the Inventory line item leads to a decrease of cash, you could consider the following:

Inventory increases → DEBIT
THEREFORE Cash decreases → CREDIT

Invent something that speaks to you.

Personally – and I cannot explain why –
I always had trouble figuring out what was the numerator and what was the denominator in the formula

Accounts receivable turnover ratio
(net credit sales / average gross accounts receivable).

Of course, I know which are the two variables that I have to relate to each other, but, in order to know which comes first, I must always tell myself the following:

"Remember that one must first sell
for there to be an account receivable."

© How to Succeed in Accounting Studies

 ❧ *Repeat, Repeat, Repeat.* When one must absolutely remember the subject-matter – or part thereof – for the purposes of an exam, repeating it is the most efficient means. Personally, "learning by heart" is the action I keep for use at the end when my learning tricks available to me have been exhausted. The idea is to read the information more than once and, under certain circumstances, to simply read it out loud. In order to better remember the subject-matter studied, certain students rewrite several times the list of steps or definitions to be remembered, for instance. You should do this if it suits your style.

When to Let Go

There always comes a time when one realizes that the preparation for an exam is complete. At that time, one realizes that the essential topics that will be assessed on the exam have been grasped. In my view, one must continue to review the subject-matter as long as this critical point has not been reached. It is not easy to explain, but, let us say that you should feel that you are ready or at least realize that you are unable to be any readier. When you can tell yourself that you have done a complete overview and that the exam could take place in the following minute, you are in the right place. Going beyond this point is not necessary, although certain students feel that it reduces their nervousness and increases their self-confidence.

Stopping before you have reached this point is risky. One last overview of the table of ratios that you have built or the sequencing of entries during the sale of an asset reinforces the knowledge you have acquired. Frequently, students stop just slightly too soon before the end. For instance, they will tell themselves that they will be able to manage if there is a question on ethics on the exam. Worse yet, they will assume that the professor will not ask a question on that topic. They then deliberately decide not to focus on the concepts of competence, of objectivity, of confidentiality and of integrity. This is a risky strategy. Has it never happened to you that the exam specifically contains the topic that you neglected?

Instead, be rather risk-averse when your training is on the line.

COMMENT

Personally, I never liked backtracking. In other words, I have always studied in order to never have to repeat an exam or a course. From this perspective, one must study enough in order to be sure of passing. Therefore, one must not stop studying as soon as one "believes" one knows enough in order to "pass" the exam. Aiming for 60% doesn't mean that you will achieve that mark.

Instead, I suggest to you that you should aim for a comfortable learning of the subject-matter covered by the exam.

By going beyond the requisite minimum,
you are exhibiting a winning attitude.

**On the day before an exam,
understanding the fundamentals of the subject-matter
greatly reduced nervousness on the day after.**

Part 4
Passing Your Exams

Planning
The Contents of the Answer
Presentation of the Answer
Feedback

« *An appropriate answer,which achieves a passing standard must contain a minimum number of relevant and fresh ideas.*»

© Deslauriers Sylvie, *Accounting for Success*
Guide to Short Case Resolution, 2015, page 58.

Part 4
Passing Your Exams

In this Part, I would like to share with you my experience, with respect to the manner of answering a test or an examination. There are attitudes, methods of proceeding, as well as tricks that may help you better "Pass Your Exams". My objective is to help you develop an examination technique in order to showcase these assets you have.

Remember, however, that this in no way relieves you of your responsibility for preparing adequately.

Planning

Upon receiving the exam itself, I suggest that you take a few seconds to plan the time allotted to you. Indeed, it is possible to arrange things in such a way that the examination will promote your success.

Here are a few items to consider.

- ☯ *Place the questions asked in sequence.* First of all, leaf through the examination in order to count the number of questions. Briefly take cognizance – very briefly even – of what you are being asked. Classify the questions according to their degree of difficulty and write the letters "D", "A" or "E" (difficult-average-easy) next to each of them.

COMMENT

For various reasons, students generally avoid starting their exam by the most difficult question. This is due to the fact that the first minutes of an examination are often characterized by a greater sense of nervousness, in light of the uncertainty of what lies ahead.

One must be conscious of the natural tendency, which is to spend a little too much time on the first few questions answered, and not enough on the last few. Therefore, do not save the most important question for last!

From the outset, one must get an idea of the time available to answer each question and sub-question. Where this information is not provided, you must estimate the time realistically. If you are not sure, allow for a timeframe (e.g.: 20-25 minutes). Take into account the points awarded for the various questions, if provided. The points awarded are not always a perfect indication of the time required, but it is still a good starting point. Where Question 3, for instance, represents 25% of the exam, you must certainly take this into account in planning your time.

COMMENT

It is not necessary to answer exam questions in the order in which they are presented. I suggest that you start with the question with which you are the most comfortable, in order to build a sense of confidence. Usually, this is a question with an average degree of difficulty.

I also suggest that you do not conclude your exam with the shortest question. Indeed, towards the end of an examination, time often is too tight, which restricts the ability to provide an adequate answer. If you have fallen a little behind – which theoretically should not happen – that is more prejudicial for a short question.

The most difficult questions, in my view, should be solved in the middle of the exam.

Of course, one must take into account the fact that the answer to a question may be a prerequisite to the following question.

◌ *Answer all the questions you are asked.* This is the best strategy to adopt in order to maximize your results. It is usually easier to be awarded the first points of a question than the last. Unless you absolutely do not know what to write, you should plan your examination in order to approach each question. Answer each of the sub-questions *(a)*, *(b)*, *(c)*, etc., if need be. If you don't know what to answer under *(b)*, for instance, you should not drop the other requirements of the question.

You must take advantage of all opportunities you are offered.

COMMENT

Where you run into a "wall" on a question, do not waste too much time on it. Some students become so bull-headed that they do not see the time fly and are then unable to solve adequately the other questions on the exam.

I suggest that you defer the questions you find bothersome to the end. You may not be able to solve them perfectly, but, at least, you will not have impeded success for the others.

It also happens quite often that solving from the outset the questions that you find easier helps you better understand those you put off till later. Also, keep an eye out for items that could be useful to you from one question to the next. It sometimes happens that a case fact in one of the multiple-choice questions, for instance, may help you solve an essay question.

Where you do not know how to answer sub-question (b), for instance, and the answer to this question is necessary in order to move on to sub-question (c), this must not stop you in your tracks. Make a realistic and reasonable assumption in order to be able to proceed and get points in the following sub-questions. In other words, try to figure out "might be" a plausible answer to (b) – even if you don't know how to achieve this result – and keep on going.

Suppose, for instance, that you are asked, under (a), to calculate the "average" ratio of the contribution margin and you have forgotten how to do so. You do know, however, that the contribution margin is 20% for product A and 30% for product Z. Hence, you should select a number between both, say 27%, since you know that the corporation sells more Z products. In this manner, you will be able to proceed and to calculate, under (b), the sales volume in order to realize a margin of $300,000. You will probably not provide the same answer as the official solution, but any adequate reasoning will be assessed and rewarded.

Any assumption presented must be plausible.

ℒ *Read the questions carefully.* Under circumstances where the time to write an exam is restricted, the natural reflex is to start writing your answer as soon as possible. It is even worse if your neighbor is already frantically pounding on his calculator.

I wish to make you aware of the fact that one must have a good understanding of the information contained in the question and place it in perspective, in the context of what you are being asked. Take the time to read, to understand and to annotate the questions in order to highlight what is essential.

Here is an example of a question that has been adequately annotated.

What is the key information?

QUESTION 3:

100!

Mrs. Sunflower, Sales Manager at Flowers Inc., is wondering if she should accept an unexpected order from one of her regular clients. The latter would like to purchase 100 dozens of roses that he would like to distribute to the women shopping at his store on Mother's Day. He offers to pay Flowers Inc. $14 per dozen roses. The usual sales price for a dozen roses is $18.

After consulting with the Production Manager, Mrs. Sunflower finds out that the variable costs and fixed costs are respectively $0.90 and $0.30 per rose. She has also determined that the delivery costs of this order would amount to $70.

100d => $70

Mrs. Sunflower is initially inclined to refuse the offer. However, she would like your opinion before making her final decision.

Required: *1.20/rose x 12 = 14.40/dozen*

(a) Explain why Mrs. Sunflower is initially inclined to refuse the offer.

QUANT
(b) From a strictly financial point of view, would you recommend that Mrs. Sunflower accept the order?

QUAL
(c) Discuss qualitative, positive and negative factors to be taken into consideration in the decision to accept the order.

N.B.: Some students highlight the words of what they are required to answer using a different color in order to make them stand out.

Referring to the previous example, I wish to draw your attention to the following points:

– Only the significant words are highlighted, within reason. As I mentioned in Part 2, I suggest that you read a paragraph in its entirety before starting to highlight, in order to avoid everything appearing in yellow. Seek to pick out the critical information, namely that which characterizes the situation you are presented with.

– A short calculation, such as the one at the end of the text portion, may help you focus the information. Here, one must note, upon reading the wording, that the reference unit is not always the same. The costs are expressed per rose, whereas the sales prices are per bunch of flowers. One must, in one way or another, remember to perform the calculations on the same basis. In the example above, since the student has decided to perform his or her calculations per bouquet, the financial information was converted on this basis. Personally, I would have made the same choice, quite simply because there is more information expressed per bouquet than per rose.

– The key words in the questions asked under *(a)*, *(b)* and *(c)* are underlined. Under *(a)*, one must note the use of the expression "initially inclined" since it appears that way in the preceding paragraph. One must, of course, pay attention to any sentence that may clarify any of the questions asked. Hence, the word "initially" may imply that the final decision will be different. That, in and of itself, is an indication that you should keep in mind, even if the rest remains to be confirmed. As for sub-questions *(b)* and *(c)*, one can note that they respectively deal with the quantitative ("QUANT") and qualitative ("QUAL") aspects of the decision.

– Finally, it is important to note that one must discuss positive AND negative factorS. The answer would not be the same if you were asked to discuss only positive factors, or discuss the most important negative factor.

Properly understanding the question asked allows one to better hone one's answer.

In addition to that which appears in the example above, I wish to suggest to you:

- to rewrite on a separate sheet each of the words of the **Required** items where you find it difficult to grasp the meaning.

- to pay particular attention to what you are being asked to do. For instance, are you required to calculate, to compare, to create a table, to criticize, to define, to determine, to discuss "*(c)*", to explain "*(a)*", to list, to prepare a statement, to prove, to recommend "*(b)*", to summarize, etc. Each action verb leads to a specific reaction.

- to draw a temporal line or a small diagram where this promotes your understanding of the information.

- to rewrite the numbers set out in the question, to be divided between sub-questions *i)* and *ii)*, for instance, in order not to forget anything.

COMMENT

Personally, I regularly jot down short notes on the examination paper itself or on a rough copy that I identify as such and add to my answer. I make sure not to forget a significant idea to be considered in the drafting of my solution later on, for instance. Since these notes do not directly form part of the answer on the exam, I write them in the most succinct manner possible. In respect of a question where I am asked what the benefits are of resorting to outsourcing for payroll processing of the employees, for instance, I might briefly write down the words "simple", "quick" and "not costly" (or "small $").

It is better to provide an incomplete answer than no answer at all!

Take advantage of the time available. Your exam is scheduled for three hours? Use the time allotted to you optimally. If, perchance, you were to finish before time is up, take the time to perfect the questions with which you had the greatest amount of difficulty. Revisiting these questions often allows you to see more clearly what is going on and to supplement your answer. Under certain circumstances, you could usefully add an idea, rewrite a conclusion or better justify a calculation. It is also possible for you to validate the result you have obtained by performing a mental calculation, for instance.

Sometimes, the little things make a difference.

COMMENT

Along the way, when they are indeed finished with a question, some students simply set it aside, upside down. Since one usually starts by the questions with which one is most comfortable, that is motivating.

Where you are not sure of your answer, clearly identify the area in question and return to it later. Incidentally, it frequently happens that solving other questions in the meantime may be beneficial.

The Contents of the Answer

In light of the limited time in which to complete an exam, one must constantly make sure to tackle what is essential. It is too easy to waste time writing ideas, which may possibly or probably be correct, but not necessarily relevant.

This is what you should consider in order to ensure that you are providing an adequate answer.

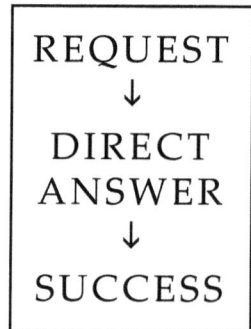

REQUEST
↓
DIRECT ANSWER
↓
SUCCESS

🖎 *Answer the question asked.* This appears to be simple; however, this is not always the case. Expatiating on all one knows on a topic may be reassuring, but it is generally not a good examination strategy. Do not go off on a tangent. If the question asks you to calculate the inventory cost, by using the average cost method, for instance, it is useless to calculate the cost using another method, simply in order to compare. If you were not asked to compare, it is a waste of time.

Do not go thinking that showing your knowledge on, say, two other methods, will compensate for your lack of knowledge on the average cost method. The points that will be awarded when your examination is marked are directly related to what you were asked. In light of the foregoing, you can no doubt infer that a very good answer to Question 4, for instance, will not compensate for a poor answer to Question 2.

COMMENT

Personally, when the answer to a question is especially long, I regularly return to read what is asked. Hence, I make sure that I do not stray from the primary objective. It would be a pity, for instance, to prepare the Income Statement in its entirety, and properly to boot, when the question only asked for the amount of the gross margin.

It is too easy to stray from what is being asked along the way. Providing your opinion to the effect that the name "Flowers Inc." is not very "in", for instance, is not really useful on an accounting exam.

---

re: p. 63   I also suggest that you balance your answers. If, for instance, you are asked to discuss positive AND negative factors, you must deal with both aspects. It would not be a good idea to discuss four positive factors and to omit those that might be negative. Instead, balance your answers between the various parts asked by discussing two positive factors AND two negative factors, for instance.

⌖ *Structure your thoughts.* Do things in proper sequence. Divide what you must do into parts or steps in order to avoid forgetting anything. For instance, prepare the template of the balance sheet by writing the name of the line items before filling it in with the appropriate numbers. The longer the answer required by the question is, the more you are required to structure your thoughts.

If need be, take a few seconds to establish a succinct outline – in writing if need be – before throwing yourself headlong into drafting an answer. It would be a pity, for instance, for you to realize that you had to recalculate the Inventory item prior to calculating the gross margin only when you have finished drawing up the Income statement. It is, therefore, useful, out of an abundance of caution, to remember the steps necessary to solving a specific aspect, even if it means skipping over a useless step.

As well, before undertaking a particularly long calculation, make sure that you determine in advance what objective you are seeking to achieve. What will be the outcome of the calculation? What is the result one wants to achieve? This helps you remain focused on what you need to do.

COMMENT

One must take into account the specific circumstances of each of the questions. A 10-point question, in a two-hour exam, should not be answered in only two sentences. Seek to identify the most important questions and ensure that you answer sufficiently in depth what is being asked.

10 points → 12 minutes

I also suggest that you survey all the information supplied to you in the question before drafting an answer, especially when there is a lot of information.

Of course, we all know that there may be items of information that are not useful, but you must also realize that there is usually a limit.

If you only use one or two numbers in order to perform your calculation, although the question contains five times more, make sure you are on the right path, and twice rather than once.

> **Whatever you do, whatever you say,
> if it was not asked, it is not relevant.**

🌀 *Learn to generate ideas.* It is not always obvious to know what to write. Running out of ideas is a destabilizing phenomenon, particularly when time is flying faster than you would like. In order to minimize this type of situation, here are a few tricks that may help you during the drafting phase.

Substantiate your ideas. Explain why you are putting forth such and such a benefit, a limit or a factor. It is rarely sufficient to merely list an item. Think of the following words: **SINCE**, because, due to, for, in light of, in order to, given that, based on, so as, etc., so as to complete your sentences.

INCOMPLETE DRAFTING

August 16, 2013

No entry is necessary.

ONE MUST SUBSTANTIATE THE IDEAS PUT FORTH.

SUBSTANTIATED IDEA

August 16, 2013

No entry is necessary because the inventory cost is less than its net realizable value.

Under certain circumstances, it is also useful to ask WHO, WHAT and WHEN. Suppose, for instance, that the question asks you to explain how the sales forecast of a car dealership can be established. The persons involved are, among others, the salespersons and the sales manager (WHO). They must estimate the number of vehicles that will be sold, per class (WHAT). This forecast may be generated for the upcoming year, after having asked the questions with respect to the budgeted sales per quarter (WHEN).

Indeed, WHO-WHAT-WHEN is not required in all cases. However, thinking of this reference guide allows you to generate ideas and to present a more complete answer.

COMMENT

In light of the previous example, I would like to draw your attention to the manner of replying to a question that asks you HOW to proceed. One must be definitive and clear when explaining how to proceed. Use examples that you know in real life. If you are asked, for instance, to explain what the components of variable costs and fixed costs are in the manufacture of an automobile, try to visualize the various steps or sequences of the assembly plant. This will enable you to provide more concrete explanations.

Consider the consequences of the arguments you are making. Considering the impact of an idea leads you to develop causal connections. Think of the following words: **THEREFORE**, hence, by way of conclusion, as a result, then, I recommend, etc., in order to develop your reasoning to its logical end.

COMPLETE IDEA

The debt/equity ratio of 77% is higher than the maximum limit set by the bank which may CONSEQUENTLY decide to recall its loan.

Illustrate your ideas by using examples. Where you are required to define or explain concepts, add concrete examples in order to illustrate your ideas. In addition to facilitating your drafting, this proves what you are arguing by demonstrating your understanding and ability to apply concepts.

ADEQUATELY ILLUSTRATED IDEA

> The operating expenses, such as an oil change and monthly tune-ups, serve to maintain the vehicles in a good state of repair

N.B.: One can generally incorporate examples in brackets in the main sentence.

Do not lose sight of what you have studied. Some students "panic" when they do not understand a question they are being asked. First of all, you should re-read the question once or twice to enable you to clarify what is being asked. If that does not work, you, of course, have the possibility of returning to it a little later.

When this happens, I suggest that you do not lose sight of what you have studied. You may not understand the question, but you must be aware that what you are being asked surely falls within the parameters of the subject-matter of the program. Do a short overview of the various topics, exercises and problems that you have studied. Also take into account what you have already been asked in the other questions. By way of inference, there is a strong possibility that you will be able to determine what the purpose of the question is.

I would also like you to remember this: try, first of all, answering a question you find troublesome in a simple manner. Unfortunately, most students do the opposite. If you do not know what to answer, refrain from embarking on complicated calculations or explanations with no end in sight.

It is easier to complete one's answer

than to recover from uselessly wasted time.

COMMENT

I take the liberty of giving you one piece of advice: do not make statements that run directly counter to what is stated in your reference volumes or by your professors. Since, for instance, everyone agrees that the "participation" of employees during the budgeting process promotes their motivation, take that for granted. This is certainly not the time, especially during an examination, to argue this point.

If a question specifically asks you to express your opinion on the topic, do so, however consider the fact that your final argument must not contradict any of the fundamental concepts. In other words, if the Finance Director asks you what you think of participative budgeting, you should conclude your discussion by stating that it is preferable.

I also remind you that you should take into account what is important for your professors. Do not overtly challenge any of their ideas. Defer this discussion to a more appropriate time.

Have confidence in yourself. It happens regularly that one or several of the questions on an exam take you by surprise. Perhaps you did not have time to review this part of the subject-matter or maybe the professor wishes to assess your analytical ability by going beyond the usual questions. Where this happens, you must realize that your colleagues are also taken aback. Then, try to present an answer to the best of your knowledge. You can certainly manage, on the one hand, by referring to basic concepts in the subject-matter tested on the exam and, on the other hand, by relying on *common sense.*

In times like these, the key concepts of your info-cards are especially useful. Incidentally, it quite frequently happens that the students clearly visualize the summaries, tables and diagrams they prepared – even down to the detail of the colors – during an examination.

Take advantage of that phenomenon.

You must find
ways to continue moving on.

Suppose, for instance, that a question on an accounting exam asks you if it is preferable to remit taxes collected on behalf of the government on a monthly or quarterly basis. And, let's say, for the sake of argument, that you have no idea! You must then seek to determine the consequences (the pros and cons) of each of the possibilities. Compare them. Think of the accounting entries. Rely on the notions you acquired in another course, if need be. Your finance professor perhaps spoke of "cash management" two weeks ago. Do not hesitate to transfer the knowledge you acquired from one subject-matter to the next.

COMMENT

Some students are so afraid of making a mistake that they water down their ideas in such a way that their answer could go one way or the other. If you do not take a stance or if there is a contradiction, your idea might quite simply not be considered by the person marking your exam.

EXAMPLE:

"I believe that it could be preferable to go with the periodic inventory system, but the perpetual inventory system might also work."

Need I even comment?

You must specify your ideas.

☺ *Consider the context.* The questions you are asked are regularly incorporated in a context that simulates a real-life situation. For instance, a question on a finance exam will use actual stock exchange quotes of a public company for analytical purposes. A decision that Mrs. Sunflower must make, as described above, is another example. Where possible, reference the context in which the Required items arise in order to explain, substantiate or discuss any of your ideas. Taking into account the facts set out in the question adds credibility to your answer.

The highlighted words are taken directly from the question.

re: p. 63

IDEA INTEGRATED TO THE CONTEXT

(c) ...

Positive factor: By accepting a special order, Mrs. Sunflower strengthens the relationship with a regular client.

N.B.: Notice the use of the name of the person in question, which adds a personal touch to the answer.

TAKING INTO ACCOUNT THE CONTEXT OF THE QUESTION

=

AN ADDED VALUE TO THE ANSWER

☺ *Knowing how to conclude one's answer.* Before moving on to the following question, I suggest that you review the question in order to ensure that you have indeed answered it. The question asks you whether you recommend that Mrs. Sunflower accept the order. You must answer clearly, with a YES or a NO, and explain why.

In addition, after having calculated a break-even point of 4,005.4 dolls, you must clearly mention that: "The break-even point in units for the new doll is 4,006 dolls." Note that, since we are dealing with dolls, a realistic answer calls for a rounding up of the result obtained.

Personally, in order to conclude adequately the answer to a question, I always ask myself if it is necessary to make a conclusion or a recommendation. If so, I set it out conspicuously, most often at the end of the answer, and I copy as faithfully as possible the words of the question itself, as in the following example.

re: p. 63   **SUBSTANTIATED RECOMMENDATION**

> (b) ...
>
> From a strictly financial point of view, I recommend that Mrs. Sunflower accept the order since the contribution margin of $250 is positive.

Ensure that your answer is plausible. In other words, make sure that your ideas or calculations make sense. It happens too often that students arrive at a number which is quite simply unrealistic, and that they continue with their answer without realizing it. For instance, a student that arrives at a variable cost of $108 per bouquet of roses should immediately stop and review his or her calculation. There was one zero too many somewhere! Indeed, the proper answer is $10.80. A bouquet of roses sold at a regular price of $18 cannot cost $108! It is not logical! Since the questions on an examination simulate real life, you should also rely on your personal knowledge.

Prior to using a number that is difficult to interpret, you should validate its plausibility.

COMMENT

When answering an examination question, you should be both focused and intuitive. Pay attention to case facts, such as "initially inclined to". Regularly assess the realistic nature and plausibility of the arguments you make.

Does it make sense?

Is it possible and feasible?

Demonstrate your practical sense!

I would like to conclude this section by issuing two warnings. During an examination, it is useless:

- *to criticize the questions asked.* What is the use of complaining about a difficult question or deeming the questions asked to be improperly structured? It is useless, except that it causes you to waste precious energy that you need in order to succeed. You must answer the questions asked to the best of your ability. Consider each of them to be an opportunity to showcase your abilities.

- *to systematically look for mistakes.* There are rarely any. Indeed, you must take for granted that the question is adequate, that is to say correct and realistic. For instance, where the question states that "…the delivery costs of this order would amount to $70.", use this number as is. Do not question it.

  Also, do not spend your time excessively looking for "red re: p. 63 herrings". Indeed, one must be wary of information that may be useless or missing, but it rarely goes beyond that. Do not approach the examination by systematically looking for flaws.

Presentation of the Answer

In the restricted timeframe of an exam, presenting one's answers efficiently is an undeniable asset. The primary objective does not change: one must present ideas that are relevant to the resolution of any question asked. However it is possible to present one's ideas in such a manner as to minimize the waste of time and to maximize success.

The following factors are what one should consider in order to present a more efficient answer.

🌀 ***Focus on content rather than form.*** It is with relevant ideas that you gain points. Hence, you must supply, by way of answer to the questions asked, the greatest possible number of ideas. Some students brighten up their text using colors or multiple underlinings. You should know that this in no way affects the result. One must be aware of the fact that the professor will not be fooled when he or she sees a long text filled with nonsensical sentences. He or she knows how to identify the relevant ideas.

Also ensure that you use, to the extent possible, terms that illustrate your ideas precisely. It is preferable, for instance, to say "The dividends to be distributed…" rather than "The amounts to be distributed…". You should avoid imprecise terms such as "thing", or "gizmo", among others. Replace them by the appropriate term. Use the glossary you created.

COMMENT

Some students occasionally hesitate to write some of their ideas because they are not certain of their validity or quite simply out of fear of appearing ridiculous. On the one hand, you should tell yourself that, generally speaking, points are not deducted for stupid answers. An idea that seems a little "bizarre" will not invalidate the rest of the answer. On the other hand, you can assume that the professor has probably seen other strange things.

Have confidence in your ideas.

Do not hesitate to write them down!

🌀 ***Go straight to the point.*** It is useless to turn around in circles by "lengthening" sentences. Presenting a long text is not automatically a guarantee of success. If you need five lines in order to express an idea whereas your neighbor only takes up two, you will be marked the same. Indeed, this is only partially true. Your neighbor will have the same result as you do for this idea, but he or she will have more time than you to perfect his or her exam. His or her ability to obtain a better result than you is, therefore, enhanced.

(a) Mrs. Sunflower was initially inclined to refuse the offer because the regular sales price of a bouquet of twelve roses is $18. I am asked to explain why Mrs. Sunflower is initially inclined to refuse the offer.

I believe that it is because the usual sales price of a bouquet of 12 roses is $18 and the special order received by Flowers Inc. from a regular client is $14 per bouquet of 12 roses. The client wishes to purchase 100 bouquets of 12 roses.

Mrs. Sunflower is initially inclined to refuse the offer, because she would receive $4 less per bouquet of twelve roses.

$$($18 - $14 = $4)$$

I must also write that the cost of a bouquet of 12 roses is $14.40, namely the total of the variable costs of $0.90 and fixed costs of $0.30 which I am multiplying by 12. I have no difficulty understanding that Mrs. Sunflower would initially be inclined to refuse it since she would sell each bouquet of 12 roses at a loss. The total cost of $14.40 is greater than the price offered by the regular client.

N.B.: Most students would present the above text in continuous, run-on sentences, without even separating the parts into various paragraphs.

187 words

Prior to presenting the list of all that "lacks efficiency" in the drafting of this answer, I wish to state that this answer is "correct", namely it contains nothing erroneous. However, the drafting of ideas can be more succinct. In so doing, the student saves time; and this time is too often restricted in the context of an examination.

Referring to the example on the previous page, I wish to draw your attention to the following points:

- The first paragraph in its entirety is useless. It is made up of sentences originating from the question and reproduced more or less as is. **This paragraph contains no new idea.** Whether or not it is incorporated in the answer changes nothing in the points awarded.

It sometimes happens that repeating the question or presenting the topic to be solved may help you understand what is being asked of you. However, I suggest to you that you do so by way of a short, clear and precise title, such as "Explaining why refuse the offer". Such a title may avoid you wasting time in summarizing, in too verbose a manner, the wording of a question.

Repeat the question? NO.
Use the words of the question at the right time? YES.

COMMENT

Some students tell me that rewriting part of the question helps them understand what is going on. In addition, while they are writing, they are able to think about what they are going to say next.

I can understand that. However, make sure that you only do it in cases of necessity and not systematically each time, simply out of habit.

Where there are no new ideas to state, abbreviate your

- The text is uselessly lengthy at times. Why repeat incessantly the expression "bouquet of 12 roses"? Simply writing "bouquet" or "12 roses" – and writing twelve in numbers – is perfectly fine. Furthermore, this sentence "The client wishes to purchase 100 bouquets of 12 roses." adds nothing to the preceding argument.

Under all circumstances – and, in particular, when you do not know what to say –, one must avoid repeating the same idea by using synonyms. An idea that is said twice, even using different words, still remains one and the same idea.

COMMENT

If you have to make an assumption in order to continue with your answer, justify it, and make it conspicuous. If you don't have the useful life of a vehicle and you are not able to establish it, make a simple and realistic assumption, and move on.

– It is also not appropriate to indicate that one is answering an exam question by writing, for instance, "I must also write...". Indeed, that is exactly what the student is doing, but he or she must not indicate it. The expression "I have no difficulty..." is useless.

I also suggest that you not write to your professor in the middle of your answer. It would be useless to say, for instance, "Sorry, I did not have time to finish..." or "Oops! I did not answer the question and I don't have time to start my answer over."

To be compared with the example on page 78.

CLEAR AND SUCCINCT DRAFTING

(a) Explaining why refuse the offer

It is normal that Mrs. Sunflower would have been inclined to refuse the offer since the price of $14 is less than the usual price of $18. She would receive $4 less per bouquet.

Also, the fact that the total cost of $14.40 is greater than the price offered of $14 is an additional reason to hesitate.

Total cost = (variable $0.90 + fixed $0.30) x 12 = $14.40

However, since it is a special order, only the variable costs must be considered, as we will see under (b).

95 words

The illustration of the succinct and clear drafting above highlights the following items:

– There are only 95 words in this answer, compared to 187 words in the illustration of the uselessly lengthy drafting! Here, the ideas that are relevant to the answer were all set out, in a much more succinct text. The last paragraph is even entirely new!

© How to Succeed in Accounting Studies

Note that it is not as easy as one would think to be direct and to use 95 words instead of 187 in order to express the same ideas. Using this example, I wish to make you aware of the uselessness of writing long sentences filled with words that add nothing to your ideas. While writing your exam, identify first of all the idea you wish to express and turn it into a sentence. Then, move on to the next idea.

I suggest also that you regularly divide your text into paragraphs. This helps in minimizing the lengthy expatiation on the same idea.

– The sentences in this example are complete: one subject, one verb and one object. For the most part, they are drafted in the present tense, in a simple style. Do not complicate your life by using the pluperfect or the future perfect tense and, if, perchance, you use the same word twice in the same sentence, it doesn't matter. What is important is that your ideas are understandable. Make sure your sentences are shorter rather than longer.

– The last paragraph is not necessary in and of itself to answer question (a). It does, however, show that the student fully understood why Mrs. Sunflower was "initially inclined" to refuse the offer. It links in to question (b), a connection that adds value to the answer.

COMMENT

I urge you to practice writing in a more efficient manner. If you are the one that the team usually designates to write the papers, it is perhaps not an advantage on an examination.

Writing the same ideas with fewer words

without skimping on what is essential

is a challenge that is worth taking up.

One idea → One sentence

82

🕭 *Show the structure.* It always appears to be easier to present an answer that is divided into parts. Have the reflex of leaving space in order to add ideas later on, if need be. On the one hand, clearly indicate that you are answering question *(a)*, *(b)* or *(c)*, for instance, and, on the other hand, indicate each of the parts of the answer by including an appropriate title or subtitle. This steers and simplifies your drafting. If, for instance, you must discuss two different means of determining the optimal level of cash, clearly indicate in the title which method you are discussing.

For instance, writing down the titles "Positive factors" re: p. 63
and "Negative factors" is a reminder that there are two segments to consider. It then becomes easier to target the answer and to adequately allot your time between the two parts. A student who does not divide his or her answer in this way risks ending up with a jumbled text which deals, on the one hand, with positive factors and, on the other hand, with negative factors, in a disorderly manner. He or she thereby increases the possibility that some of his or her ideas will be incomplete. Under the circumstances, it is also more difficult to assess the balance in discussion between the two aspects.

> **COMMENT**
>
> Students get into the aggravating habit of wanting to answer all parts of a question simultaneously.
>
> This is not a good idea.
>
> It is generally better to divide one's answer into several parts, even if you make connections between them a little later on, if need be.

🕭 *Presenting one's calculations adequately.* One must ensure that one provides calculations that are understandable. Take a step back, and examine the manner in which you usually present your calculations. Is it difficult to identify the beginning or the end of what you are doing? Are the numbers placed in a space that is so restricted that it is difficult to read them or to establish a link between them? Spreading them out, among others, helps the reader understand. The same goes for the use of round and square brackets where indicated.

Some calculations are so incomprehensible that it is difficult to see where they end up. I suggest to you that you should always indent the result you obtained, and clearly indicate what it represents. This is all the more important where it is measured other than in dollars ("$"), such as kilometers or liters.

It sometimes happens, as well, that students do not explain where their numbers come from. Where the professor is unable to understand the reasoning followed, you will understand that it is difficult for him or her to give you points, even partially.

re: p. 63

INCOMPLETE DRAFTING

(b) ...

$$??? $$
$$[(\$14^* - \$9) \times 100] - \$70^* = \$430 \text{ of profit per bouquet}$$

* These figures come directly from the question.

The origin of the $9 is not explained. That is very unfortunate, especially since the final answer is not the right one. Since the $9 amount does not appear as such in the question, unlike the numbers $14 and $70, it is necessary to know where it comes from in order to reward – at least partially – the reasoning shown. Incidentally, several additional explanations would have to be provided as to the reason for the quantitative approach decided on.

Indeed, I could "think" that the student multiplied the variable costs of $0.90 per rose by 10 instead of 12. **If one assumes** that this is indeed the error that the student committed, this means that the notion of contribution margin was properly understood and applied. You will understand, however, that the person marking the exam cannot be absolutely certain thereof. The $9 amount could just as well be the result of the reverse phenomenon, namely an inadequate use of the concept.

Do not ask the person marking your exam to extrapolate on your behalf the reasoning underlying your answer.

**If it is not written,
it is difficult – if not impossible –
to assume what was done.**

Make sure that you explain each of the numbers used, especially those that do not originate directly from the question. Where you do not wish to overburden your line with numbers, use the references ⓐ, ⓑ, ⓒ, etc., and provide brief explanations a little later on.

Do not waste time explaining the origin of numbers that are directly supplied in the question, unless the same number appears twice, which is rather rare.

USELESSLY LENGTHY DRAFTING

(b) ...

$0.90 of variable costs x 12 roses
= $10.80 of variable costs per bouquet of roses
$14.00 sales price - $10.80 variable costs per bouquet
= $3.20 of contribution margin per bouquet
$3.20 per bouquet x 100 bouquets
= $320 of total contribution margin
$320 of profit - $70 of delivery costs = $250 of profit

There is no mistake, everything is there… and even a little bit too much! There are several useless repetitions. It is as if the student had written all that was running through his or her head, word for word, as he or she was progressing through his or her calculations. Some words are too often repeated and the "$" sign does not have to be written as often. It is also not necessary to provide all the subtotals. Finally, words that are an integral part of our field could be abbreviated, such as "CM" which stands for "contribution margin".

(b) ...

variable costs $0.90 / rose x 12 = $10.80 / bouquet
net contribution margin:
(($14 - $10.80) x 100 = 320 - delivery 70) = $250

I recommend acceptance of this order for 100 dozen roses,
because the profit it generates is $250.

I wish to conclude this section by issuing three warnings. During an exam, it is useless:

- *to use a question style.* An idea that ends with a question mark is not sufficiently precise. A sentence such as, "Should I recommend that Mrs. Sunflower accept the order?" is wholly useless. Since you are being asked to answer the questions, you can certainly not direct them to others.

- *to change the instructions.* Where you are instructed to write nothing on the overleaf, for instance, why would you do otherwise? Or else, when you are required to perform the quantitative part with calculation software, why make the extra effort of doing it with word processing software? Follow the instructions at all times and, please, wait for the appropriate moment to give your opinion.

- *to cross out one's ideas.* In the heat of the action, it is easy to misjudge the value of what one is writing. Do not cross it out just in case. Place the text in brackets and write the word "draft" next to it.

Feedback

The result obtained on an examination is, of course, the first thing you want to know. Although you may have some idea of this outcome at the end of the exam, it is normal for you to want to officially validate your impression. Aside from the result in and of itself, I suggest that you analyze your answers in order to be able to minimize your weaknesses and to maximize your future success.

This is what I suggest.

🖎 ***Understanding your errors.*** It goes without saying, but I know that too many students skip this step allegedly because the subject-matter that has just been tested is generally not retained for the following exam. As mentioned previously in this volume, understanding the concepts underlying the current topics makes it easier to understand those that follow.

When you analyze your answers to an examination, you must identify and understand why you lost points.

Where did you go wrong?

There are, in my opinion, two types of errors to be distinguished:

1- *Inadequate understanding of the concepts.*

It appears to me to be crucial to obtain promptly the necessary explanations in order to understand what was missed. Perhaps you improperly applied a concept or, otherwise, the result of your exam shows that you did not understand it at all. It may also be that you unfortunately neglected to perfect your study of one of the topics on the agenda of the exam. Regardless of the number of points that this may have cost you, make sure you understand the reason for your mistakes without exception. A 3-point question today may be the basis for a 16-point question tomorrow. Therefore, do not hesitate to clarify the situation by asking your professor or your colleagues.

2- *Errors due to distraction or mistakes in calculating.*

It is understandable that you might commit this type of mistake in a context where you are nervous. If there are a lot of these types of mistakes, do not neglect this signal and try to find ways to better manage your stress.

**Do not let an uncomfortable situation last.
Try to find a solution.**

COMMENT

A student who was very successful in his or her exam is, rightly so, very proud of his or her success. Indeed, he or she may tell himself or herself that he or she understood the fundamental concepts that were assessed.

I would like to suggest to this student to nevertheless take the time to analyze his or her exam or to listen to the explanations of the professor with respect to his or her solution.

> Was the answer drafted efficiently?

> Was the reasoning presented logically?

> Are there areas where points were awarded, but barely?

There are always things that can be improved and – who knows? – perhaps it will make a difference during the next exam?

⟲ ***Know how to take advantage of experience.*** Take notes on what you must take away from an analysis of your examination. For instance, you might go and supplement your summaries and info-cards. This exercise could also lead you to realize that your manner of studying the subject-matter can be improved on. Perhaps you do not devote enough time to the presentation of the transactions on the financial statements, for instance.

In Part 1 (p. 12), I suggested, incidentally, that you collect separately, in the same place, all the tips and advice with respect to how to succeed in your studies. Personally, right after writing an exam or following the analysis of my answers, I would write immediately any observation that I should recall for the next time.

One could, for instance, note the following comments:

- *Answer all the questions!*

  "You know the answer, so try at least to write down the most important ideas, even if you have to go faster. At least take the time to write the outline of what you wanted to say."

- *Be positive!*

  Saying "I do not recommend that you rent this equipment" is not the same as saying "I recommend that you purchase this equipment, because…".

– *Diversify your answer!*

"There are two buildings, therefore it is practically certain that there were differences between the two. The professor rarely asks the same thing twice."

– *Ideas must be precise. One must provide meaning!*

Writing "It is advertising." is not sufficient. One must write something along the lines of "Flowers distributed on Mother's Day are a good way of advertising one's business."

– *Distinguish between a fact and an opinion!*

Stating that "The working capital ratio is 0.75." is a fact. Stating that "The working capital ratio is too low compared to the industry." is an opinion! More points are awarded for the second sentence.

COMMENT

Following an analysis of the results of an exam, I suggest that you determine what was your greatest strength and what was your greatest weakness. Knowing how to recognize what is going right is motivating. On the other hand, being able to determine what stood in the way of your success can bring you to determine as soon as possible how to correct the situation.

Also look at whether you can improve your methods. For example, a student who realizes he is wasting time attaching accounts and their amounts to the right financial statement will develop a trick to speed up his approach. When dealing with a trial balance, for example, he might decide to highlight all the accounts in the profit and loss statement (statement of net profit) in blue, and then those of the statement of changes in financial position (the balance sheet) in green. When the time comes to draw up the requested statement, he will be faster, while again ensuring the accuracy of his classification.

Acquiring knowledge is a continuous process.

Part 5
Working As A Team

The Exchange of Ideas
Grading Responses Amongst Colleagues
Written Papers

"The challenge is to find a balance between individual and group work."

Part 5
Working As A Team

In our profession, "Working As A Team" is unavoidable.

The Exchange of Ideas

All throughout your learning process, I strongly urge you to consider the possibility of exchanging with your colleagues. Such a practice, in addition to adequate individual preparation, is a guarantee of success, especially for significant or complex topics.

Here are the activities that I suggest.

  ℰ *Explaining the subject-matter to others.* This is one of the best ways of crystallizing one's own understanding of the concepts under study. Providing an all explanation forces you to structure your thoughts and to express them using appropriate words.

  Students who explain the subject-matter to their colleagues are in a win-win situation. In addition to the personal satisfaction of being helpful to others, their own understanding of the subject-matter improves. I can also add that listening to the explanations provided by someone who does not approach things in the same manner allows one to examine concepts from a different angle.

COMMENT

It appears to me to be particularly useful to exchange between colleagues in the context of preparing for an exam. However, it goes without saying that any of the activities of advance study, as described in Parts 2 and 3, can be conducted in a team environment. Two friends, for instance, can do some exercises together. After having sought to solve a given exercise, they can exchange their impressions and discover the answers to questions that arose. In addition, it is often useful to see how a colleague absorbs and retains information.

Personally, I consider that any student must perform the bulk of his or her study individually. Indeed, the effort expanded in learning on one's own, among others, allows one to identify more precisely what is not going right. Within a group dynamic, it is not as obvious to identify what one's own weaknesses are. One must, therefore, at some point in time, confirm one's own understanding of the concepts as well as one's ability to apply them. One must also consider the fact that each and every one finds himself or herself alone when comes exam time.

As far as I am concerned, any activity synthesizing the subject-matter under study should, first and foremost, be an individual effort. In other words, you should first attempt to summarize the subject-matter, create tables or diagrams, draw flowcharts, supplement your glossary or draw up info-cards. Secondly, sharing information with your colleagues enables you to enhance your work and to reinforce the knowledge you have acquired.

Exchange information between colleagues?
MOST CERTAINLY.
Secure the work of another without any effort?
ABSOLUTELY NOT.

COMMENT

It is especially interesting and useful to exchange on critical items making up a given topic. To this end, the info-cards you have created are very useful.

Revisit all the key concepts forming part of a topic.

Recall the steps to follow.

Prepare a list of items required for a certain type of calculation.

Exchanging with your colleagues greatly facilitates the retention of the subject-matter in the program.

☺ *Ask yourself questions.* It appears to me to be both interesting and motivating to go through the exercise of asking each other questions. Ask your colleague the definition of this or the benefits of that. List to your colleague explain the differences between a private enterprise and a public company. Or, instead, do an overview of the tax rules on the various taxable benefits that an employee can receive. And, finally, try to generate examples that will enable you to distinguish entertainment expenses from advertising expenses.

If you were the teacher, what questions would you ask?

Personally, I consider it to be very useful to imagine what type of questions may be on the exam. I am not referring here to questions that are akin to the exercises and problems contained in your reference volume. Rather, I would like you to appeal to your imagination in order to ask yourself, amongst colleagues, in which new fashion such and such an aspect of the subject-matter could be asked. For instance, instead of being asked to calculate the interest expense, you could instead be provided with this amount directly, as well as the interest rate, and you could be asked the extent of the liability at the beginning of the period. Preparing for the unpredictable teaches you to develop your capacity to react rapidly and properly to any different or new situation.

COMMENT

I suggest to you that you seek out examples illustrating the concepts that appear to you to be more difficult to grasp. Make analogies with situations that occur in real life. For instance, discuss amongst colleagues the notion of "economic order quantity" (EOQ). Seek to visualize this concept for a restaurant, for instance, a toy manufacturing plant or a furniture store. In addition to reviewing the why and how of the EOQ model, discussing it from a practical point of view reinforces your ability to use and interpret it adequately.

Indeed, it is quite possible that the exam will not be structured at all in the manner of the scenarios that you can conjure up. However, knowing how to reply to questions asked in a different manner stimulates your analytical mind and confirms your understanding of the subject-matter. The risk of being destabilized or surprised by an exam question is then reduced.

© How to Succeed in Accounting Studies

> ## Exchanging ideas between colleagues helps reduce nervousness prior to an exam.

Grading Responses Amongst Colleagues

I suggest that you regularly ask one of your colleagues to assess what you are doing from a quantitative point of view AND from a qualitative point of view. Select an exercise or a problem, solve it, and then ask your colleague to grade it while you do the same for him or her. Knowing that your answer will be read and assessed by another person simulates exam conditions to a certain extent.

The purpose of grading amongst colleagues is to objectively identify your strengths and your weaknesses in developing your answers. Knowing the subject-matter is one thing, knowing how to answer exams in an efficient manner is quite another. This assessment among colleagues must, therefore, go beyond the contents as such and also venture into the presentation of ideas.

Here is a list of attitudes to remember when you are practicing this activity.

- *Be objective.* A person grading your exam reads the words that are written, black on white, without adding or removing any. Indeed, he or she cannot assume what the other person intended to say. In other words, he or she may not complete the answer where an idea is not clear or a number is not explained. Indeed, one must realize that a person marking the paper does not assess directly the knowledge of a person but rather the knowledge that he or she committed to paper. There is often a gap between the two and grading amongst colleagues allows one to highlight such a situation.

> ## The assessor evaluates the written words, no more and no less.

How is this impact negative?

BECAUSE?

Write a complete sentence!

re: p. 63

(c) Negative factors

- impact on current clients

N.B.: Here, words are missing that would enable the person grading the answer to understand the precise and complete meaning of the idea. He or she can certainly not add them to the student's sheet!

COMMENT

Grading amongst colleagues is a good opportunity to check if your writing is legible. Some students write in very small handwriting or barely form their letters, which, then, all appear similar. Others use a whole range of signs and abbreviations that no one but them recognizes. Finally, some people use a style that is too telegraphic, making it too difficult to grasp ideas.

Do not lose sight of the fact that the person grading your exam must understand what you have written without experiencing any difficulty. Nothing must slow down the reading process. Make sure that he or she focuses on the contents of your answer and not on the container. Under the circumstances, I remind you that spacing out the answer or the calculations in your answer promotes the understanding of the reader.

◉ *Be constructive.* The purpose of this activity is to help you mutually to improve your manner of replying. Therefore, it is not sufficient to criticize but you must suggest solutions or other manners of proceeding. If you find that the idea is expressed in too general a fashion or that the substantiation of the result obtained is incomplete, tell your colleague what is missing.

The synergy resulting from the sharing of ideas is very stimulating.

- *Be creative.* When you grade the answer written by one of your colleagues, be creative. For instance, you could cross out all the useless words in a long passage or write ⓡ next to words that are too often repeated or sentences that revisit an idea that you have already floated. Incidentally, do not hesitate to use signs such as "?", "!" and "+/-" which briefly indicate what needs to be said.

ANSWER ANNOTATED BY AN EVALUATOR

Be sure of Yourself!

...

~~I believe that~~ several documents are necessary to perform a bank reconciliation.

COMMENT

One of the benefits of grading amongst colleagues is that it enables you to see different ways of writing. Hence, you may observe a style of writing that is more efficient than yours.

Your colleague, for instance, may have presented the lists of benefits and drawbacks in the form of a list indented from the margin. This is a good idea, which you should recall when you are asked to supply a "list" of items.

Another may have created a three-column table for financial analysis by way of ratios: the formula of the ratio, its calculation and its interpretation. This is a good idea, which you should remember when you wish to classify information based on repetitive criteria.

Finally, when you use the terms "budget of receipts and of disbursements" as a synonym for "cash flow budget", it was a good idea. Your colleagues may remember it when they cannot remember precisely the term to use.

Not everyone learns the same way.

Here are other examples of comments that could be written on the answer of the colleague that you are grading.

- "You must take into account the case facts provided in the question. Everything is expressed in weeks, so you should express the final results in weeks."
- "Your conclusion is very clear. Super job!"
- "You could write PP&E instead of Property, Plant and Equipment in order to go faster".
- "The expression *going around in circles* is not appropriate."
- "You are not answering the question. You were asked to suggest means in order to improve the situation. Instead, you explained why there was a problem.

  That is not the same thing!"

Written Papers

It sometimes happens that preparing a written paper is part of the requirements for passing a course. This regularly takes the form of simulations where, for instance, various business transactions must be recorded in the accounting records. Let us also mention stock exchange simulations or preparing a business plan.

Most of the advice contained in this volume is still valid, such as the need to answer each question, for instance.

COMMENT

Some students systematically discard the work they are asked to do which counts for few points. In other words, they do not do it. You will not be surprised to read that I do not concur with this strategy. On the one hand, each item of work you are asked to do, regardless of the points it is worth, is useful to your learning. On the other hand, 3 points, for instance, can be the difference between a B+ and an A−. Furthermore, the points you are able to glean when writing papers are generally easier to achieve – that is to say less uncertain – than exams.

This is what you should remember when you are asked to submit written papers.

- *Follow the instructions.* When preparing a written paper, you must consider the fact that you have the time to fine-tune it. Spelling and grammar mistakes, which may be overlooked during a written exam in a restricted timeframe, must be avoided. Indeed, you must submit the work properly, in keeping with the instructions of the professor and according to governing rules. It would be very unfortunate to lose points on aspects of presentation that are easy to control.

- *Form a coherent whole.* This is quite a challenge, especially where several students divide the tasks amongst themselves. In an ideal world, the content of the work is basically performed as a team. In reality, in light of the busy lives that each person leads, this is not always possible or efficient. Out of experience, I consider it to be at least necessary:

  - That the planning of the work – a detailed plan of what needs to be done – be the result of the participation of all. One must also schedule regular meetings in order to assess the situation and review the division of tasks if need be.

  - That a process of mutual review of the work performed be provided for. In other words, the work performed by each of the team members is read and commented by at least one other member of the team, and so on.

  - That a designated person – or even two – conduct a final review in order to ensure that the work consists of a coherent whole. This should not, however, relieve this student from doing his or her part in connection with the contents as such.

Different parts → **Single job.**

The professor should not be able to distinguish the various parts drafted by different students. The parts of a written paper must, therefore, be sequenced in a logical manner and fit seamlessly together, without any contradictions or useless repetition. One must, therefore, take the time to establish connections between them.

> **Showing respect for oneself
> and one's colleague
> is a key success factor in any teamwork.**

◎ *Re-read the paper prior to the exam.* It forms an integral part of the program underway. Since it is quite often an application of the concepts in a specific context, re-reading the paper forms part of the "things to do" in order to prepare for the exam. This is all the more useful where you did not directly work on any of its parts. If you did not participate in the entry of the payroll in the Payroll journal, for instance, you must definitely review this part prior to the test on adjusting journal entries.

I wish you all a great SUCCESS and
Thank you for appreciating my work.

www.ingramcontent.com/pod-product-compliance
Lightning Source LLC
Chambersburg PA
CBHW071435210326

41597CB00020B/3806